The Secret World
of Drawings

Marie-Louise von Franz, Honorary Patron

**Studies in Jungian Psychology
by Jungian Analysts**

Daryl Sharp, General Editor

The Secret World of Drawings

A Jungian Approach to Healing through Art

GREGG M. FURTH
Introduction by Elisabeth Kübler-Ross

National Library of Canada Cataloguing in Publication Data

Furth, Gregg M.
  The secret world of drawings:
  a Jungian approach to healing through art

2nd ed. Originally published by Sigo Press, Boston, 1988.

(Studies in Jungian psychology by Jungian analysts; no. 99)

Includes bibliographical references and index.

ISBN 0-894574-00-1

1. Art therapy.
2. Drawing, Psychology of.
3. Jungian psychology..
I. Title. II. Series.

RC489.A7F87 2002   616.89'1656   C2001--901283-7

INNER CITY BOOKS
Box 1271, Station Q, Toronto, ON M4T 2P4, Canada
Telephone (416) 927-0355 / Fax (416) 924-1814
Web site: www.innercitybooks.net / E-mail: admin@innercitybooks.net

Honorary Patron: Marie-Louise von Franz.
Publisher and General Editor: Daryl Sharp.
Senior Editor: Victoria B. Cowan.

INNER CITY BOOKS was founded in 1980 to promote the
understanding and practical application of the work of C.G. Jung.

Cover illustration by Jessy, age 12.

Index by Vicki Cowan

Printed and bound in Canada by University of Toronto Press Incorporated

This book is dedicated to all who contributed their drawings and shared their life situations. Their contributions are unusual—for us they will make real the content of what lies within the secret world of drawings.

Table of Contents

Foreword

G regg Furth has written a book which finally makes the very rich tool
of picture interpretation available to therapist and layman alike. A
student of mine and of the British analyst Susan Bach, Gregg Furth
has perhaps more knowledge of and talent in this field than anyone cur-
rently working in the United States. Although both my work and that of
Susan Bach concentrate on drawing as a means of communication with the
terminally ill, Gregg Furth has expanded the technique into the realm of
everyday therapy — that is, with people who are not necessarily dying, but
who nevertheless are helped by expressing what is on their pre-conscious
minds through spontaneous drawings.

As Gregg Furth mentions in his book, spontaneous drawings are one
of the most radically effective yet accessible tools at the analyst's disposal.
Such a drawing takes but a few minutes to create, and all the materials needed
are paper and a few colored pencils. The drawings can be made anywhere,
from a hospital bed to a school desk, and as a source of psychic information
they are just as effective as dreams. Unlike dreams, whose interpretation
demands years of intensive training from the analyst, valid spontaneous
picture interpretations can be made by any responsible and compassion-
ate person — a teacher, minister, doctor, etc. — as long as he conscientiously
follows the guidelines Gregg has provided us. The method was originally
developed around the therapy of terminally ill young children, whose ca-
pacity for abstract verbal expression is not yet fully developed and thus who
are most open to the symbolic means of communication represented by
spontaneous drawings. Gregg has shown that drawing is also very effective
with adults, disturbed adolescents, and the siblings and parents of very

ill children. The therapist working with spontaneous drawings will find not only that this is a very useful analytic tool indeed, but also a powerful one. Moreover people enjoy drawing and will go about it with a level of enthusiasm often lacking in other therapeutic situations — simply because it taps into the universal need to express oneself.

Gregg's book is based on themes first raised two decades ago by Susan Bach and Jolande Jacobi. The patient is handed pencils and paper and asked for an impromptu drawing. A picture develops within minutes. Like dream-language, the language of pictures is the language of the unconscious, and it speaks when the conscious voice fails.

The drawings allow for an interplay of information between the various expressed or repressed areas of the individual psyche. The analyst establishes a rapport with his patient that goes beyond conscious interaction to include an unconscious dialogue between his intuition and the often secretive unconscious language of pictures. For this reason, however, proper training is absolutely essential, since the analyst's tendency to project onto a drawing often goes unrecognized by both him and his colleagues. That training completed, professionals are capable of generating helpful and therapeutic picture interpretations, to the immeasurable benefit of both interpreter and drawer.

Another very fruitful aspect of Gregg's picture interpretations is what I call "preventive psychiatry." Gregg points out again and again, especially in the poignant case study in his Introduction, that somatic ailments can sometimes be covertly expressed in unconscious pictures weeks, months, or even years before they are actually diagnosed. Unconscious pictures thus can be an effective diagnostic tool (although Gregg cautions against over-emphasizing this aspect of his work) as well as a purely analytic one.

The Secret World of Drawings is being published at a particularly auspicious time. The psyche/soma interaction mentioned above has been gaining tremendous medical support over the last few years. In Europe and the United States, the sandplay technique has seen a recent resurgence in popularity among analysts; once again an indication that the concrete representation of psychic contents is becoming an increasingly well-understood theoretical and therapeutic phenomenon. Finally, thanatological studies are gradually transforming our views on death, which we no longer have to consider a fearful and mysterious pathological occurrence, but rather an integral stage in the individual's psychic development. This is especially important in context of the dimensions that cancer and AIDS have assumed in our society: with the help of Gregg's technique, we can now reach out to those suddenly faced with their own mortality or the mortality of others close by, not only establishing valuable therapeutic communication with them, but also allowing their unconscious fears and emotions to become conscious, and thus to be confronted and resolved.

Elisabeth Kübler-Ross

Preface

I am very glad that Gregg Furth has written this book, which is distinctive because the whole field seems to have been overlooked in the psychological literature. This is particularly surprising in context of analytical psychology, given that the reality of pictures is granted an especially important position within Jung's conception of the psyche.

One of the primary reasons for this silence may be the anxiety, shared by analysts and lay-readers alike, that arises whenever we are asked to methodically examine psychic material. Doesn't every instruction in picture interpretation run the danger, one might ask, of violating the autonomy and complexity of psychic expression? Doesn't the very act of drawing, as well as the accompanying experience of freedom and creativity, provide so much of an effective therapeutic impulse that one could do without the psychological analysis? And doesn't interpretation destroy the psychological and emotional benefit of drawing, a benefit gained by escaping the strictures of consciousness and allowing oneself to grow through play and creativity?

It is well known that there exist members of the helping professions who, because of such considerations, or because they question the value of preconscious symbolic expression, deliberately renounce attempts at spontaneous picture interpretation. If they do not allow their patient to draw, they are stifling his means of communication, especially if the patient's ego is unstable because of youth or pathology. If they allow the patient to draw, yet refuse to interpret the drawing, then they are contradicting a natural need of whoever has drawn the picture — he is enthralled by his creation and wants to understand its meaning. This need is entirely appropriate and inherent to the nature of the symbolic, which represents a synthesis between sensual reality and the appearance of a sense; between form and meaning; between a beauty which touches and a truth which concerns.

Interpretation can paradoxically help discover a particular kind of beauty in a drawing. Whoever has made a drawing often judges his picture according to external aesthetic criteria, and he therefore tends to underestimate it in view of his limited means of pictorial expression. Here, interpretation can help the patient change that viewpoint and those criteria. Namely, it allows him to experience that, deep inside, his unconscious is allowing for a surprisingly accurate expression of his emotional state of mind; this, in turn, allows the patient to experience the deeper knowledge reigning beyond his conscious intentions. In the end, it is only interpretation that permits the patient to change over from subjective opinions on the actual aesthetic creativity of his drawing to a better understanding of the autonomous psychic reality it expresses. In this sense, interpretation in no way leads to a reductive summary of the picture, but rather to amazement — on the part of the patient as well as of the therapist — at the wisdom of its fundamental creativity.

Gregg Furth eminently succeeds in conveying this feeling of respect towards the drawings he discusses, while at the same time inviting their methodical exploration. He lets the reader feel that picture interpretation is both a mysterious game and scientific work. In this sense, his book is a superior introduction to the right spirit and competent practice of picture interpretation.

Dr. Paul Brutsche

Introduction

There is very definitely a scarcity of information on the use of drawings in a psychotherapeutic context, and this is especially true for information on the use of drawings in work with physically ill patients. My initial attempts at using drawings to help in the therapy of somatic ailments were frustrated by this lack of information. I thus had to turn to related projective techniques such as the Draw A Tree, the House-Tree-Person, Draw A Person, and Kinetic Family Drawing exercises, and soon realized that they were insightful indicators of both psychological and somatic information about the person drawing.

My initial doctoral research revealed that important unconscious psychic contents were conveyed in drawings not only by the seriously ill, but also by the healthy, those whom we call "normal" individuals, both psychologically and physically. If this unconscious content is deciphered, it provides highly valuable therapeutic insight. Not only did I discover that drawings reveal information about the individual who executes them, but I began to understand that the information gleaned from the same drawings could apply to others as well, especially to the members of the patient's family.

I will begin with the story of how the unconscious world of pictures first made itself powerfully clear to me, and how the process of picture interpretation helped not the person who drew the picture, but his closest family member instead. This case is a preview of what *The Secret World Of Drawings* is all about — a means of deciphering and understanding drawings as insights into an individual's psyche at the time of the drawing. I will present this case as it was presented to me and subsequently developed. This book is in effect an explanation of the process which led to my discovery of the unconscious information revealed by this particular drawing.

When I was living on the West coast several years ago, a colleague telephoned to ask if I would analyze a drawing. My colleague requested that I take on the task with no questions asked. Knowing that my colleague could be trusted implicitly and that she must have had a very good reason for that last stipulation, I consented. A few days later a cylinder containing the drawing arrived in the mail.

Fig.1
(Also see Fig.95, page 123)

I looked at the picture briefly and returned to my other responsibilities. A few days later, I was called by a woman who very courteously informed me that it was she who had sent the drawing on the advice of my colleague. I said that I had received the drawing and that I had already spoken with our mutual contact. I then asked about the drawing,

who drew it, and the person's age at the time. The woman replied that
she understood I was to decipher the drawing with "no questions asked,"
as it were. We concluded our conversation and made an appointment for
the following week. An hour later, my colleague from across the country
called back to reiterate that I ask no questions, but trust her and decipher the drawing. I merely told her that I was going to meet with the
mystery woman the following week.

Then I went to work on the drawing in a definite way. As I pondered
the picture over several days, I became increasingly haunted by it. I decided
to keep the drawing, which was good-sized, about three feet square, on
display so that I could examine it daily.

My position on picture interpretation is generally that no single focal
point is conclusively indicative of what is happening within a patient's
psyche. A series of drawings with all their focal points needs to be as-
sessed before it is possible to make a diagnostic or prognostic evaluation.

Nevertheless, in this case I had to begin somewhere. I noted what feelings the picture evoked in me, and realized that I did not like many of
them. My impressions ranged from tiredness, agony, encapsulation, to
a feeling of old age. I considered it important to keep these impressions
in mind as I worked on the drawing, since those feelings must also have
been experienced by whoever had drawn it. I tentatively determined that
the drawing was by a child near the age of five, since drawings can reflect
developmental stages, and this drawing is what I would have expected
from a child of that age.

It seemed most likely that the child was a boy, and that he was suffering from a terrible illness which had invaded his body cavity and possibly infected his head as well. I intuitively sensed that he was frustrated
not only by his illness, but also by being held back from doing the things
he wanted. I wondered what was happening in his environment that was
blocking him, or rather, who in his life was doing this to him. Very naturally with a dying child, it could easily have been his mother, and other
evidence in the picture supported this idea (see Chapter Six). The evidence, however, appeared to be contradictory. In some ways the child appeared as if he did not want to be held back, yet in another way it seemed
that he knew the restraint was acceptable and necessary. The child did
not vent his anger about this inner ambivalence, but rather seemed to
be repressing it.

I was curious about the appearance of the nose in the drawing, since
it seemed disjointed for a child who was obviously capable of an accurate
depiction of other body segments. I wondered if this could be interpret-
ed as a difficulty with the breath of life, or even a spiritual concern with
his father, or with God? This idea came to me because the nose obviously has something to do with breathing, and breath is an important symbol of the soul, the life-giving power, the *spiritus mundi*. The throat and

neck region was next on my list, since it was obviously exaggerated and distended. I wondered what his illness or what the medical world had done to his throat in somatic terms. I also wondered what this distortion could mean psychologically.

From the expression on the figure's face, I asked myself what purely psychic needs the child was trying to express. It seemed the child was already seeking and moving into the next world; yet he was also still here in this world. If we look at the figure's eyes, we can see that one eyebrow is raised in a quizzical manner, perhaps suggesting amazement and surprise. The figure's right shoulder blade has a definite red marking much different from anything else in the drawing.

What somatic phenomena did all these anomalies indicate? The child appeared unable to contain himself, so to whom did he look for containment and support? Was his mother his compensatory side? Many questions were running through my mind, and I was looking forward to the upcoming appointment with increasing curiosity.

When I finally met the woman, I welcomed her into my office, where I of course had the drawing available. We introduced ourselves and discussed our mutual acquaintance (the colleague who had referred her to me). I broached the matter of the drawing by asking two questions — the age and gender of the person who had drawn it. Her immediate response was resistance, and she reminded me that I had agreed to interpret the picture without asking questions. Of course she was correct, and I told her so, but I also told her that I thought this meant not asking questions concerning history, and that I had to know the sex and age of the child in order to produce any sort of valid interpretation. I also wanted to know what her relationship was to the child.

After more resistance from her, I told her that I could follow one of two courses. First, I could decipher the picture non-committally because I did not know who drew it, nor her relationship to that child. The picture, as do all pictures, consisted of materials which are confidential, and I wasn't sure if she had an ethical right to know them. Second, she could tell me what I wanted to know, and with that information I would have fewer qualms about the interpretation. A bit reluctantly, she agreed to the second course, but asked me to promise to tell her all I could decipher. I said I would share the appropriate information as we worked together on the drawing, and she accepted this.

She told me that she was the child's mother, and that he was her firstborn child, a son five and a half years old when the picture was drawn in a preschool class. I also learned that the boy had later died and that the woman had a new baby only a few months old. She was delighted that this second child was a girl, since this helped her resist the temptation of treating her second child as a replacement for her son. She also informed me that she wanted to learn from the drawing because she did not want to repeat the ordeals she had undergone with him.

I told her that I had determined from the drawing that her son had experienced a serious illness in the body cavity. She confirmed that it was true, that her son had died of retroperitoneal sarcoma, a cancer of the inner peritoneum. He had been operated upon in the stomach region. The illness lasted about nine months. I asked if the cancer had metastatized to the brain, to which she answered no. I was surprised, but I didn't push the point further. I said that I felt the boy had been in some way held back, and she readily agreed. She knew that her relationship with her son had been very close and that she had been very protective. In one respect this was good to hear, for the dying child needs to know that his parents are protective and ready to do all that is possible to help him. I was convinced from the drawing that the boy had felt the warmth and love of parental protection. On the other hand, this protectiveness can often become a heavy burden. This is one dilemma of parenthood — how much love is appropriate and not overburdening and damaging to a child? It is so difficult for a parent to determine when protectiveness is beneficial and when it is counterproductive.

I couldn't help but think about the woman's husband. What was their relationship like? She spoke of her husband and his work. She free-associated and told me stories from her own childhood and particularly emphasized the age of six, even though it did not fit in directly with what we were discussing. I asked her what happened to her at that age and she told me that her father had died. Her brother, a year and a half older than she, had a close relationship with their mother and was the favored child. As a child the woman had felt left out, abandoned, so to speak. I wondered if she had married in an attempt to find a father-image, but she denied it when asked. Upon meeting her husband, however, I noted that he was several years older than she.

She admitted to her anxiety and fear of rejection in her relationships with others. "It's safe to put up barriers," she said. With her son she felt that she did not have to do so. She felt free with him, very close, perhaps even over-possessive. She was conscious of her possessiveness and was brave enough to be willing to look at its negative side in order to avoid a similar error with her second child. The son's obvious bravery in facing his illness seemed very much like his mother's bravery in looking into her own dark side. I wondered whether he had learned this from her, or she from him.

She told me she was a nurse and had decided to take her son home from the hospital. She felt strongly that she could do as much for him at home as they were doing for him there. In some ways this did curtail his freedom, because she wanted him to conserve his energy. She limited his play and did not want him to try to do too much, all with the great hope that a cure might be available in the not-too-distant future. She did feel that her son was frustrated by this, but the picture reflects that he restrained his anger.

The boy's illness was diagnosed in March, 1974. In June, when he was no longer able to retain food, it was decided to maintain his nutritional balance through hyperalimentation, which requires the insertion of an intravenous line into the patient's bloodstream. Note the dark red line in the child's upper right shoulder (Figure 1); this would be the usual point of insertion for intravenous feeding. In November he developed an intestinal obstruction, and in early December a suction tube was inserted through his nose to drain gastric secretions. Now we can understand the distorted nose on the face in the drawing. In mid-December a tracheotomy was performed to ease the child's breathing. The elongated neck, very unusual in young children's drawings, could express the passing of a tracheotomy tube through this region. The boy died nine days later, on Christmas Eve. The drawing emphasizes the child's somatic as well as psychic experiences throughout his illness. I hope his parents found some comfort in the Christian belief that "it is fortunate to die on Christmas Eve, for the gates of heaven are wide open then" (de Vries 1984, p. 131).

What is most remarkable and most unusual is the fact that the picture was drawn ten months before the child's diagnosis. This is a forecasting picture in every sense of the word, with insights into the disease in terms of both psyche and soma.

When I concentrated on the face of the figure in the drawing, I saw the face of an old man, and we may wonder about this. But is anyone really "young" when so near death? I have seen many dying patients young in years but old in spirit as they prepare to leave this world. In my opinion, I see the "wise old man" in the patient's psyche leading him on his way, and that is somehow deeply reassuring to me.

As should be apparent, drawings in general, and especially this particular one, express tremendous amounts of information about unconscious psychic contents. It appears that there is a direct link, at the unconscious level, between psychic and somatic pathologies; thus when the unconscious "speaks" in a drawing, it very often expresses potentially disturbing somatic anomalies that the conscious mind is either unprepared to face or unable to understand. In terms of preparing individuals for their own deaths or for the death of a loved one, which is exactly the kind of holistic psychology Kübler-Ross is advancing, unconscious pictures can be of invaluable aid, especially by allowing the dying person or his loved ones to confront the finality of death with honor, so to speak, and not with the loneliness and isolation we all too commonly witness in nursing homes or wards for the terminally ill. This information helped the child's mother to live with a fuller understanding of her loss and, in turn, to prepare for a new way of living. She became conscious of having, to some extent, stifled her son, and she was thus better prepared to prevent this from occurring with her second child. Her greatest comfort was that the drawing showed that something in her son "knew" what was happening and what was going to happen — it was his journey, his task, and although painful to both him and her, she knew that his life was in fundamental harmony with some higher source.

This book, then, is at root a suggested method for deciphering the language of pictures. As the reader proceeds, he will discover how the unconscious contents of this picture were made known to me as the student of the picture.

Before concluding this Introduction, I would like to add a few general comments about format. The words *picture* and *drawing* are used interchangeably. I have selected the words *patient* and *therapist* to maintain a standard phraseology throughout the book, but the terms should be considered as referring to two individuals working together with unconscious materials. The use of the word *therapist* should not imply only psychotherapist. Alternative pairs could be client/counselor, analyst/analysand, etc. . .

Two categories of drawings are discussed. I have defined them as spontaneous drawings and impromptu drawings. Spontaneous drawings are from individuals who begin to draw on their own and not because they are asked to do so. Impromptu drawings are executed on request, on the spur of the moment, without preparation, and can either be in free style or on a selected topic.

The contents of the drawings in this book speak for themselves, though I have changed names, family situations, country of origin, and content when it is not relevant in the interpretation of the particular focal point under discussion. The drawings have been collected over the past sixteen years of my work in this field, and the content of each was very significant to the patient at the time of the drawing. In no way do the drawings indicate each particular patient's psychic situation today, since each patient has perhaps worked through the material and it thus no longer occupies an important place in his or her psychology.

Throughout this work, the pronoun "he" will be used to indicate "patient," unless of course the patient has already been identified as female. The usage is unfortunate, since it seems to exclude at least half of humanity, but it is a necessary convention.

Gregg Furth

CHAPTER 1

DRAWINGS AS EXPRESSIONS OF
THE UNCONSCIOUS

To cure sometimes,
to help often,
to comfort and console always.
Anonymous

Many current theories in the interpretation of art have evolved largely from ideas generated in the work of Carl Jung. He emphasized the importance of symbols, and one way symbols manifest their significance is through drawings from the unconscious. Through such drawings we come closer to the use of symbols as a healing agent. This agent is both psychologically and somatically involved in the development of what Jung calls the "individuation process."

Building on the pioneering work of Carl Jung were Jolande Jacobi and Susan Bach. Jung saw value in drawings containing symbols from the unconscious that could work as a healing agent, although he did not present any means of analyzing drawings for their unconscious content. Jolande Jacobi took on the task in her *Vom Bilderreich der Seele* (1969), in which she attempts for the first time to teach others about the interpretation of pictures. Susan Bach went further in her book *Acta Psychosomatica: Spontaneous Paintings of Severely Ill Patients* (1969), not only demonstrating that the unconscious contents in drawings can be deciphered psychologically, but also that through them, the unconscious can empirically project what is happening to the body.

This book is different from the writings of Jacobi and Bach. My intent is to present a more practical approach, including some basic focal points

1

on how to decipher drawings, along with illustrations of these focal points in order to better understand certain psychological and somatic events within the individual. These will not be rules or recipes, but guides to understanding the unconscious content manifested in pictures.

Freud spent three weeks in 1913 studying Michelangelo's statue of Moses, measuring it, sketching it, until he could capture an understanding of it. Then he wrote more than twenty pages on his interpretation of this work of art, which he saw as a symbolic representation of deeper aspects in the sculptor's psyche. Perhaps this is an important lesson for those of us who wish to interpret pictures: one must spend time with the picture, study, measure, and even trace and redraw the picture, noticing how much time and energy goes into different parts of the drawing. It seems that when physical energy is expended, psychic energy makes itself more easily apparent.

In Jung's conception, the realm of the unconscious, collective or personal, can be represented in art through images and symbols. These images and symbols are displayed in paintings, sculpture, poetry, dance, music, literature and many other forms, and are expressions coming from the creative side of the human being. This content originates in the unconscious, the seat of creativity.

Images from the collective unconscious are archetypal, and they meet us in dreams and fantasies, in myth and religion. When they arise, we are often "touched" somehow, as if we know they belong to us, that they are true, and that they carry a meaning we cannot explain. Understanding and realizing that the symbols in drawings may come from the collective level of the unconscious aids us in answering specific questions related to pictures and their interpretation.

Aspects of a Complex

It is necessary to be somewhat familiar with the make-up of a complex in relationship to picture study. Complexes, both positive and negative, arise from the unconscious and often manifest themselves in a drawing. A positive complex is not usually why a patient seeks a therapist, so discussion here will be limited to so-called negative complexes.

We must remember that unconscious material originating in the psyche will remain in the psyche while manifesting itself externally in outer world difficulties, as if to say to consciousness, "Look at me! I am here!" These difficulties and adaptations appear symbolically in drawings or in dreams. Following the symbol, we approach the complex in which the problem is intermingled and we allow the energy connected to the complex to flow. Since the energy can no longer remain stagnant, it begins to flow as we encounter it, and it can then be brought to consciousness.

I illustrate this with a drawing (Figure 2) by John, age 37. We see his family decorating the Christmas tree. The scene looks festive and joyful in many ways. Under the tree we count eight gifts, one for each person. However, there are only seven people in the picture. Who is missing? First John replied that "There is no extra present. I just put a bunch of presents there." After counting them John said, "I guess it's for my father." Fourteen months later I talked with John again. During the intervening time he had been working with his therapist. He told me the drawing of the Christmas tree picture "was leading information which began one year of working on the relationship with my father. This was a real unblocking experience." The drawing was a memory of John's when he

Fig. 2

was five years old. The complex was buried deep within his psyche, and manifested itself unconsciously on the drawing paper. The five-year old in the picture is now thirty-seven and has a better understanding of himself in relationship to the internal image of his beloved lost father, who died when John was an infant.

In dream analysis, some images and symbols illustrate a connectedness to a complex or, at least, one aspect of the networking of a complex. The complex lies in the unconscious and we know dreams can come from this level. Furthermore, we know that complexes are discovered through analysis of pictures from the unconscious as well as from dreams. We can conclude that if dreams and pictures from the unconscious reveal complexes, then they both touch the same level of the unconscious. Consequently, one can say that working with complexes can bring about growth and development of an individual psyche and that this work can be accomplished with art therapy.

Psychic Energy and Redistribution of Psychic Energy

We frequently hear the term *libido* used in the field of psychology.

Freud's interpretation of libido is different from Jung's. Freud described libido as psychic and emotional energy associated with instinctual biological drives, sexual desires, and a manifestation of sexual drives. By *libido* Jung meant psychic energy, "the intensity of a psychic process, its psychological value" (Jung 1976 CW 6, pg. 455-456). Fundamental to Jung's concept of libido are the energic phenomena of progression and regression. As an analogy, Jung compares the progressive nature of psychic energy to the flow of water. Essentially, water that is flowing cannot be stopped. Water flows from a higher level to a lower level. In theory, if sufficient water collected and the water backed up, we would have a regression. The water could be channeled elsewhere, or the water could be stored, eventually reaching a maximum level and of its own accord flowing off into a new direction. This is seen psychologically as progressive movement.

There must be both a progression and a regression of libido. Opposites exist, producing a balancing effect. Without one the other does not exist. If something advances in one direction, then it diminishes from the other. This is Jung's *principle of equivalence,* which he expresses by citing Ludwig Busse: "For a given quantity of energy expended or consumed in bringing about a certain condition, an equal quantity of the same or another form of energy will appear elsewhere" (Jung 1978, CW 8, pg. 18).

Citing Busse further, Jung claims that "the sum total of energy remains constant, and is susceptible neither of [sic] increase nor of decrease." This is Jung's *principle of constancy.* We become aware that an individual has a fixed level of psychic energy. This energy is not growing and gaining in size, but is invariable and constant.

A therapist needs to be alert to the flow of energy from a patient's unconscious. This can be ascertained through pictures from the unconscious as well as in analysis without pictures; however, pictures are direct communications from the unconscious and cannot be as easily camouflaged as can verbal communication.

Fig. 3

The principles of equivalence and constancy are demonstrated in an example of a working woman who is married and has three children. Her psychic energy could be distributed as illustrated in figure 3.

One quarter of her psychic energy goes to her husband, her relationship with him as a man in her life and as the father of her children. One quarter of her psychic energy is devoted to the children and their bond with her as their mother. Her profession demands one quarter of her psychic energy, leaving one quarter remaining for herself and her growth and needs.

What happens to the distribution of psychic energy when a blockage or difficulty arises? For instance, if her husband dies, the husband quadrant is suddenly empty. The psychic energy from this woman to her husband drastically decreases. More energy goes elsewhere. At first the loss of the husband still devours her psychic energy to some extent, but with time this diminishes. The woman has to deal with new allocations of psychic energy, such as becoming both mother and father to the children, or devoting more attention to her profession in order to meet increased financial responsibilities. This all coincides with mourning the loss of her husband. The new distribution of energy is seen in figure 4.

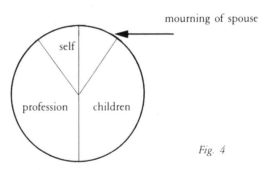

Fig. 4

We find more psychic energy is devoted to the now fatherless children. More psychic energy is directed towards the woman's profession. At one time this woman felt that with both her husband and herself working, they could reach the goals they had set for their children's education. With his unexpected death she begins to feel pressure to advance in her profession, hoping to obtain more security and thus better provide for her children. With this increase of energy directed to the children and her profession, a corresponding part or parts must regress. In this example, and far too often in reality, mourning for her husband – and her Self – are the parts that diminish.

When an individual has to take on a burden such as a tragedy, what normally happens is that the person ceases participating in nonpriorities and reallocates energy in order to handle the burden. What at one time was thought important is now set aside under the new load of carrying a different, perhaps more tragic burden. The redistribution of psychic energy is important to the balance of the psyche. Under these circumstances one, of course, never gets more than one can handle, because the psyche re-assigns priorities and a redistribution of energy comes into play to allow for handling the new burdens. Of course this does not happen only in the event of tragedy. It can take place because of a new love, a job promotion, or any change where a shift in psychic energy is involved.

In terms of relating this directly to the use of pictures and picture interpretation, the therapist and patient can ascertain from focal points in drawings where psychic energy is located. The therapist working with the patient discovers whether this energy is flowing or blocked. In either case, together they note its status and attempt to follow its future path. When the patient works on the issues involved with the blockage, then the psychic energy begins to flow again.

This brings to mind an important question which Jolande Jacobi raises in her book. She asks if "it is not better to carry out the 'art therapy' independently and dispense with analytical discussion" (Jacobi, 1969, pg. 50). Of course this must be answered by each analyst in the particular course of analyzing the patient's inner and outer situation and psychological attitude. As with dreams and dream analysis, caution needs to be observed. In a deeper sense this question is about psychic energy and its path.

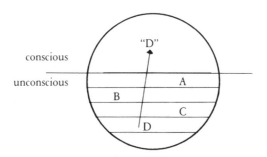

Fig. 5

Dora Kalff (1981), a Jungian analyst who has done much pioneer work in the use of the sandtray for therapeutic purposes, conducts little analytical discussion with patients. She allows the sandtray activity and the unconscious of the patient to work independently of any logical explanation. She demonstrates that the sandtray (and this is true of drawings as well) allows the deep regions of the unconscious to move into consciousness as needed. The conscious and unconscious experience unencumbered interplay and dialogue.

An illustrative diagram may show this interchange and dialogue more clearly. If the sandtray or drawing goes to a level (see figure 5) of the unconscious D, then by analytical discussion of issue D we are dragging this particular item through different levels of the unconscious and bringing it directly into consciousness.

As we see in the diagram, items C, B, and A are closer to consciousness than D. Being the furthest away, D does not have the urgency of item A. As a therapist who trusts the unconscious, I see that item A is more ready to surface. However, item D unconsciously manifests itself in the sandtray or drawing. Allowing it to be played or drawn out activates its psychic energy enough to raise it sufficiently and bring about the domino effect. This would move C upward, thus advancing B upward and allowing A to flow into consciousness. This is illustrated in figure 6.

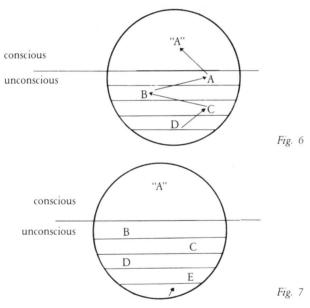

Fig. 6

Fig. 7

As this occurs, the unconscious immediately reorganizes, and being a "bottomless pit" another item, E, appears. See figure 7.

Theory of Opposites

Jung believed that "the psyche is a self-regulating system," and that "there is no balance, no system of self-regulation, without opposition" (Jacobi 1980, pg. 53-54). Opposition allows for balance; it creates tension and from tension emerges energy. The greater the opposition, the greater the tension, the greater the energy available. If we rid ourselves of the opposition, we rid ourselves of the tension, and thus we diminish the energy available to us as well. With energy the human being can go about taking on tasks in life. Many individuals in our society see it their goal in life to be tension-free. In a tension-free status, there is no life, only existence. The force to live, if we can call it that, comes from opposition, the tension between the opposites, the magnetic pull and push. Jung uses the term *enantiodromia* to describe this phenomenon; specifically it is "the view that everything that exists turns into its opposite" (Jung 1971, CW 6, pg. 426).

Theory of Compensation

Jung's theory of compensation is based on his theory of opposites. A therapist should not try to impose any particular behavior upon the patient, but rather must be willing to accompany the individual's unconscious on its journey. Believing the psyche to be a self-regulating system that is balancing and adjusting itself as necessary, the therapist follows the patient's unconscious as it deals with life. Jung's theory of compensation suggests that the unconscious either complements or compensates the conscious, thus always striving for balance.

We know that parapraxes (which are referred to in more detail in Chapter Two) and dreams have unconscious roots and are frequently not in alignment with conscious intent or attitude. We can conclude that dreams, drawings, and parapraxes are independent and exist in their own right. Jung refers to this as "the autonomy of the unconscious." The content from the unconscious does not owe loyalty to the conscious world. It does not follow consciousness exactly and sometimes may even place itself in flagrant opposition to it. When the unconscious content coincides with the conscious world, we say both worlds complement each other. They have a resemblance and they may even reflect each other. They harmonize.

Compensation is different, as it implies opposition to the conscious world, and brings about a balancing effect in the psyche. It is often important for the therapist to know the patient's conscious attitude in order to understand the compensatory attitude of the unconscious.

It is important to discover what the dream message means to the individual, to guide him or her in the direction of the greatest potential for growth. Through compensation, the unconscious may reveal some important factors for the individual to consider and incorporate into his life. Similarly, in drawings it is important to discover whether a picture compensates or complements the psyche. Then it is important to see what the person can learn from this information.

An example is an individual who is easygoing, amiable, has no ego identification, is sometimes "tred upon", and thus may become, at times, angry at an unconscious level. This person never displays his anger, but remains silent. He then reports dreams of fighting, bombing, and physical violation of other dream characters. These dreams would be seen as compensatory; they compensate for his overly-passive conscious attitude and keep his psyche in balance by allowing the energy of the anger to flow. In releasing the repressed anger, more of the whole person is expressed. On the other hand, if an individual is a traveling salesperson, always going to another meeting in a new city, continuously flying around the world, and then dreams of boarding an airplane to travel somewhere, the dream is complementary and coincides with the dreamer's conscious world.

The aim of analytical psychology is to learn what the unconscious is saying and to raise it to the level of consciousness — in short, to become more conscious in every sense of the word.

Role of the Symbol in Healing

A symbol from the unconscious always acts in a compensatory or complementary relationship to the conscious status of the psyche at a given moment in life. If the conscious attitude is one-sided, so involved with one aspect of life as to exclude another, then this compensatory energy emerges as a symbol from the unconscious. A compensatory symbol expresses the neglected area, either in a dream or fantasy or in a drawing, in an attempt to bring it to the attention of consciousness and promote a change in conscious attitude. The neglected area always demands attention in some way. Thus the symbol has a healing influence, striving for balance and wholeness.

A symbol refers to something so deep and complex that consciousness, limited as it is, cannot grasp it all at once. In this way, the symbol always carries an element of the unknown and the inexplicable, that which is not amenable to words, and which often has a numinous quality. Yet the very fact that the symbol exists tells us that at some level we know or feel the meaning behind the symbol. In this tension between knowing and not-knowing, between conscious and unconscious, there is a great deal of psychic energy.

Consciousness is analogous to focusing the eye. The area of peripheral vision is the unconscious which needs to be brought to consciousness. The symbol is a vehicle for bringing peripheral vision into focus, aiding the movement of psychic content from an unconscious level to consciousness. This potential for consciousness is what makes human beings different from other animals, for with this potential we can understand ourselves, even at the deepest levels, and make conscious decisions about our actions and the direction of our lives.

In the religious and mythological realms, symbols play an important role. The symbol, of course, represents an aspect of religious belief or a mythological motif, and it carries the psychic energy of that belief. It can even incorporate "faith healing" when the believer comes into contact with the power the symbol is carrying for the individual. Activation of this power is the healing process.

Jung wrote that it is the archetypes, universal and inherited psychic patterns, that constitute and structure the unconscious. Of the image he writes:

> I call the image primordial when it possesses an archaic character. I speak of its archaic character when the image is in striking accord with familiar mythological motifs. It then expresses material primarily derived from the collective unconscious, and indicates at the same time the collective rather than personal. A personal image has neither an archaic character nor a collective significance, but expresses contents of the personal unconscious and a personally conditioned conscious situation.
>
> The primordial image, elsewhere also termed archetype, is always collective, i.e., it is at least common to entire peoples or epochs. In all probability the most important mythological motifs are common to all times and races (Jung, 1976 CW 6, pg. 443).

Archetypes set a pattern for both psychic and physical life. Myths, legends, dreams, and pictures are some of the means by which archetypes "travel". A myth may carry a universal belief found in all religions. Myths survive from one generation to the next, both for their historical value and as an educational tool to help people find direction in life. In many religions, a ritual enacted around the telling of a certain story is maintained, thus providing a universal belief system, history, and education to its followers (Harding 1961, pg. 8).

Whether the Gospels, for instance, were really written by Mathew, Mark, Luke, and John is no longer debated; instead it is generally assumed they were not. Nevertheless, Gospel as legend has a ritual function in the Mass. Even today, with other prayers and readings in the Mass taken on by lay persons, the priest remains the reader of the Gospel. The special words serve historical, educational, and healing functions, and their redemptive power is, within a Christian context, essential to further spiritual growth and development.

The symbol unlocks unconscious psychic energy and allows it to flow toward a natural level, where a transforming effect occurs. With more psychic energy available and flowing, the individual encountering a difficulty now has the possibility of pulling unconscious elements into consciousness, dealing with them, and thus transcending the problem. The problem no longer has the individual, but instead the individual has a hold on the problem. The external problem may still be present, but it is now understood differently, and this can make a world of difference.

For example, consider the way an individual might carry a physical burden. If it is carried in a suitcase, then the carrier's hands are filled and occupied. However, if a person carries the burden in a knapsack, both of his hands are freed for other tasks; in each situation, the individual carries a burden, but the approaches are different and thus the results as well.

Fig. 8

How do we activate the healing power of the symbol? First of all, we need to bring it into consciousness and to allow its connected energy to flow. Spending time with a symbol invests energy into its flow. Drawing it, writing about it in a journal, or bringing its associations and amplifications to consciousness are means of accomplishing this.

Esther Harding very accurately answers the question of how to activate power from the symbol to obtain healing:

> It seems that for a reconciling or redemptive symbol to be fully effective four conditions must be fulfilled. First, the individual must be deeply concerned over his need; second, he must have struggled to the utmost of his ability to find a conscious way out of his dilemma; third, the symbol itself must express the life process of the unconscious, active in this particular individual; and, lastly, he must grasp the meaning of the symbol that is presented to him, not only with his mind but with his heart also, and must act upon its teaching (Harding 1961, pg. 17).

Art versus Pictures from the Unconscious

Let us differentiate between pictures from the unconscious and art as produced by the world's great artists. In both creations, the content derives from similar layers of the unconscious. Pictures from the unconscious represent primitive, raw material taken directly from the unconscious, undeveloped, yet filled with the unconscious content closely connected to the individual's complexes. Naturally, some of these pictures from the unconscious could be great masterpieces. However, artists creating their works of art use their creative power, both conscious and unconscious, their world of opposites, in a total way to produce works of art.

For the artist, the masterpiece is the culmination of conscious and unconscious development, the result of years of observation and study of artistic technique, as well as personal experience that may or may not be consciously remembered, along with the innate psychology of the artist himself, and of course including his connection to the collective unconscious. Thus the masterpiece speaks not only for the individual psyche, but also, in deeply unconscious ways, for the collective psyche.

Both the artist and the patient drawing pictures from the unconscious may be prompted by inner necessity. What would Michelangelo, Picasso, or Dali have done had they been forbidden to paint? Perhaps society would have had to institutionalize them. Artists need to paint; they seem unable not to create. The situation is no different with all individuals; few can refrain from "doodling" in meetings, during long telephone conversations, and so on. The artist within feels a compelling need to produce, and these productions are representative of the individual's psychology.

While the artist is interested in aesthetics and technique as well as the drawing or painting's feeling tone, in pictures from the unconscious all considerations but that of feeling tone are irrelevant, since the value of the pictures is in the psychic expression itself. Naturally, the pictures from the unconscious that we ourselves draw have more of a feeling tone related to them, since aesthetic considerations in these cases are less important than the power of activated unconscious elements.

It is interesting to note that when professional artists produce pictures from the unconscious, they frequently become aware of a flow of inner good feelings accompanying their work. They seem to be expressing a freedom that they have not felt in years, or awakening memories of using media associated with good feelings experienced years ago. Pictures from the unconscious executed by artists, interestingly enough, are awkward and childlike, even primitive, and the drawings are very similar to those by non-artists. Any drawing has a cathartic effect, and that catharsis allows the symbol to move inner psychic energy and begin the healing process.

When pictures emerge from the unconscious, they bear a tremendous amount of psychic information. Through the picture we can follow the journey of the psyche and where it is at the moment of the picture's inception. The idea is not to decipher with accuracy what is within the picture — in order to predict the person's future — as much as it is to ask concise questions as to what the picture may be communicating. This communication lays bare the unconscious and its energy. If we want to follow the unconscious, we need to consider its suggestions and enlightenments, and so bring the individual into a greater state of consciousness.

CHAPTER 2

PREMISES—WHAT ART THERAPY
"STANDS" ON

*It is as difficult for a man to see himself
as it is for him to look behind himself
without turning around.*
—Thoreau

To know ourselves, we need to bring into consciousness what is submerged in our unconscious. Our unconscious thoughts come through to us in the symbolic language of dreams, paintings and drawings. A systematic analysis of drawings, very similar to dream analysis, can further understanding and awareness of these messages from the unconscious. Not only do dreams and their drawings enhance our development, but fantasies and imaginings from the waking state as expressed in drawings also reveal conditions of the various parts of one's total personality, mind, and body. The use of drawings, dreams, fantasies, active imagination, or a combination of these forms of symbolic communication broadens self-understanding. Through analytic interpretation of these expressions we learn to recognize our weaknesses, fears, and negative traits, as well as our strengths, accomplishments, and untapped potential, giving us greater insight into who we are.

Learning about our own psychology, we discover our own developed and undeveloped sides, and how to avoid projecting those hidden sides onto others. In learning and experiencing our individual psychology, we become better prepared to help others travel the road to self-discovery. This is the *wounded-healer theme:* if I can face my wounds and work toward healing, then I am better prepared to help another face his wounds and work toward his healing. We can never accompany another person beyond where we have traveled ourselves. I am not saying that only a horse can judge a horse show, but it certainly helps to know something about horses before going about judging them.

Looking at a picture with no preconceived ideas may be difficult, yet we must try to take the picture at face value and see how it fits into its creator's life. When we come with this openness to a picture, we do not so easily project our own psychology onto others. This projection is the greatest danger of all: that is, to come to a picture with preconceived ideas, to believe that another person's psychology is the same as our own. An open mind is vital to the productive interpretation of a drawing and to helping a patient follow his own path, not the path that we think he should take.

There are three premises we must accept in order to understand the language of drawings. The first is that there is an unconscious, and that pictures come from the same level as dreams. We are individuals who resemble the iceberg in figure 9, with only a small part visible and the rest submerged. In the iceberg illustration we see a representation of conscious and unconscious content.

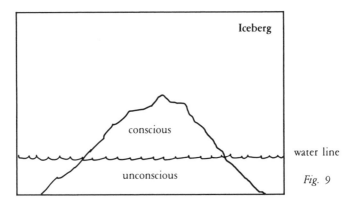

Fig. 9

Included in this premise of accepting the existence of the unconscious, where pictures and drawings originate, is the need to consider other important signals coming from the unconscious and revealing themselves in our drawings and lives. Information from the unconscious may present itself in our daily lives as an accident, or as Freud termed it, a parapraxis.

By parapraxis, then, I understand the occurrence in healthy and normal people of such events as forgetting words and names that are normally familiar to one, forgetting what one intends to do, making slips of the tongue and pen, misreading, mislaying things and being unable to find them, losing things, making mistakes against one's better knowledge, and certain habitual gestures and movements. All of these have on the whole had little attention paid to them by psychology; they have been classed as instances of 'absent-mindedness' and have been attributed to fatigue, to distracted attention or to the contributory effects of certain slight illnesses. Analytic enquiry, however, shows with enough certainty to satisfy every requirement that these later factors merely operate as facilitating factors and may be absent. Parapraxes are fullblown psychical phenomena and always have a meaning and an intention. They serve definite purposes which, owing to the prevailing psychological situation, cannot be expressed in any other way. These situations as a rule involve a psychical conflict which prevents the underlying intention from finding direct expression and diverts it along indirect paths. A person who is guilty of a parapraxis may notice it or overlook it; the suppressed intention underlying it may well be familiar to him; but he is usually unaware, without analysis, that that intention is responsible for the parapraxis in question. . .If a person's attention is drawn to a blunder, the next thought that occurs to him provides its explanation (Freud 1913-14, *Collected Works of Sigmund Freud*, Vol. 13, pg. 166-167).

It is noteworthy to focus upon this particular occurrence because it appears frequently in drawings. We need to look first into what these "accidents," or parapraxes, are. Behind every supposed error or accident lies a repression. Something directs psychic energy elsewhere than our consciousness intends at the moment the accident occurs. In picture analysis, we do not want to push aside markings on drawings simply as accidents or errors.

Recently a woman who was involved in a car accident told me that someone had veered into her car, yet she admitted she could have avoided the accident. She mentioned during analysis that her brother always had his way, even if she were the deserving one. Here, we discovered through a car accident an individual saying, "I had the right of way, so why should I get out of the way all the time?" She still feels the hurt of having to "get out of her brother's way" in the family, and in this case she acted those feelings out by not stopping her car—even to avoid a collision.

An incident that happened to a friend provides another good example. One day this friend had to attend a meeting at a university in Los Angeles. Mrs. X suggested to him that they meet at her hotel room before the conference to discuss the agenda and my friend's presentation. When he arrived in Los Angeles, he found he did not have the room number of the hotel, nor could he recall Mrs. X's name. He remembered the name of the hotel and knew that if he took a taxi directly from the airport he could meet her on time. He had known Mrs. X for several years, seeing her once or twice a year, and was sure her name would come to mind on the way. However, to his frustration, he arrived at the hotel still unable to recall her name or room number. He could not ask the desk clerk at this very large hotel for the name of a woman of such and such a description. He considered phoning a friend back home, asking the friend to go to his apartment to search for his date book and give him the details; but at home it was 5 A.M. (he lived in Europe). He passed the reception desk and found a comfortable, conspicuous seat in the lobby, thinking Mrs. X might appear to search for him. After he sat down and calmed himself, he thought: "I forgot her name and room number; I left it in my date book on my desk at home. This is not like me; this is an important meeting. What made me do this? Why don't I want to meet this woman?"

He thought he had liked Mrs. X, but he immediately realized that he didn't like being alone with her. Then he had to ask himself what was it about her that caused him to want to avoid being alone with her. The answer came to him. It was because she needed to feel attractive to all men, and he was sure that she had her company arrange their meeting in her hotel room. His intuition told him that she wanted to "get him into bed" the way she had done with two of his colleagues. She might then spread rumors, and my friend did not want this. Then an interesting thing happened. Having analyzed his problem of forgetfulness to this point, he immediately recalled her name and room number. Next, he thought of what he could learn from all this and decided on what he wanted out of their meeting, went to the desk, and asked the clerk to phone Mrs. X to tell her he had arrived and was waiting for her in the coffee shop. He was a few minutes late, but certainly more conscious and more aware of his feelings.

These anecdotes illustrate that perhaps accidents, errors, forgetfulness, slips of the tongue, and slips of the pencil stem from the unconscious. They are the result of repressed fears and anxieties. Frequently the question is asked whether some aspect of a drawing is the result of an "accident" or of the drawer's poor artistic ability. The accident theme is illustrated above to help the reader understand more fully that we must look for the meaning behind every "accident."

We evaluate a drawing by comparing one of its particular features with the whole drawing; in other words, by looking at the drawing in terms of its internal anomalies. For example, we sometimes find human figures drawn without hands. The artist says that he cannot draw hands, yet we notice facial features and clothing appropriately detailed in the drawing. Having ascertained that the artist is able to draw faces, clothing and shoes in detail, then we know that he also has the technical ability to draw hands. One wonders what it is the person is repressing, or what is missing in his life that the hands—or the omission of hands—symbolize to him.

Of course the therapist needs to determine what particular symbols mean to the patient and must not jump to generalizations on the meanings of symbols. In order to discover what may lie at the deeper levels in an individual's psyche, the meaning of a symbol must be defined in terms of the individual's own private symbolic language.

"Accidents" in drawings or the " involuntary" drawing of something different from what was planned by the conscious mind is illustrated below. A woman's personal experience with an impromptu drawing reflects the later development of an organic condition. A few years ago, Laura, age 33, was asked to draw an impromptu picture. At first she resented the request, but realizing that she was attending a workshop on picture study and that very soon she would be asking others to make drawings as a part of her doctoral research, she decided to cooperate. She considered it a good opportunity to gain insight into her own forthcoming study (Figure 10).

She intended the drawing to be a portrayal of herself in the room in which she was then seated. Although there were approximately sixty people in the room, the drawing portrays no one but herself.

From a psychological point of view, the drawing raises several ques-

Fig. 10

tions. The individual is seated inside an empty room holding onto the end of a couch that is large enough for more than one person. How is it that this person left the place next to her empty? Is she feeling very alone and lacking the support of intimate friendship?

Close examination of the couch reveals that the portion of the couch closest to the center of the page, that is, the empty portion of the couch, is faintly drawn. Does the empty, faded portion of the couch represent an underdeveloped half of this person? The woman portrayed in this picture has no breasts and no feminine characteristics. In addition, her right hand covers her genital area. How complete has been the development of the feminine aspect of her personality? Lacking legs on one side, the couch could not possibly support her, and this may be further reason to question the fullness of her development as a complete person.

When the drawing as a whole is viewed as an expression of the person who produced it, one notes the striking difference between the portrayal of the indoor and outdoor portions of the drawing. Four windows span the width of the page in the upper quadrants. Outside these windows are many trees and a rising sun. However, the form of the trees is quite indistinct and one sees only chaotic lines outside the windows. Could it be that emptiness and isolation characterize the inner life of this person, while chaos characterizes her outer life — even though this outer life may be filled with potential riches? The woman titled the drawing "Beginnings of Peace," suggesting the presence of positive elements in her life.

Certain characteristics of the figure in the drawing raise similar questions about the contrast between her inner and outer life. The shoulders are drawn with very heavy lines and extend out wider than would be expected. A very broad smile covers the face. Can it be that she presents a smiling face to the world while inwardly she feels overburdened?

The woman who drew the picture reported that, after examining it, she became very aware of how accurately the drawing reflected her situation and feelings at the time. Just about a year into intensive psychoanalysis, she was becoming aware of the extent of the despair, pessimism, alienation, and sexual inhibition that had characterized her life up to that time. Busily occupied with a full-time psychology internship, a part-time psychology assistantship, doctoral classes in psychology, and work on a thesis, she presented a competent smiling picture of herself to those around her, but she was acutely aware of feeling that she had no time for herself. She struggled with her feelings of being unlovable but did, at least, have the support of feeling that she was beginning to find herself professionally.

From a somatic point of view, one can ask if her right hand covering her genitals represents a need for her to protect this area of her body. She later recalled that she had intended to portray her right hand resting on her thigh. As she drew, it was as if "involuntarily" her hand ended up protecting her genital area. "I distinctly remember being surprised that I could so misjudge the distance I'd intended to move the pen," she said. At the time, the significance of this occurrence was lost to her, and she laughingly commented to me about her sexual inhibitions as she handed me the drawing.

One year later she wrote informing me that she had gone to her gynecologist for a routine examination. The results of the test were positive. The Pap smear indicated cancer, and a biopsy confirmed the diagnosis.

Here we have an excellent illustration of someone involuntarily drawing something into a picture. Some would call it an accident, some would say it could be due to the lack of artistic ability, but, at a deeper level, it is significant in terms of the individual's personal psychology and physiology. Other such cases are illustrated in Chapter Four, Guidelines, and in Chapter Six, Case Studies.

After accepting the presence and function of the unconscious, the second of our three premises is that the picture must be accepted as a valid method of communicating with the unconscious and as conveying its meaning reliably. *Reliability* in a picture specifically means that the content is trustworthy, it keeps working time after time, more or less for all people at all times. It is dependable, and the therapist can use it as a reliable analytic aid in helping the patient grow and develop. *Validity* in a picture means that it shows (or tests) what it purports to show (or test), e.g. repressed or undeveloped psychological contents, which are rich and relevant. In brief, the content of a picture is always supported by, and is well grounded in, actual fact. This perspective, of course, comes from the patient. We are always working from the patient's perspective of his reality; that is, as he perceives it to be.

The following case illustates the damaging effect of not accepting drawings as a valid and realiable means of communications. Three figures were drawn by a sixteen-year old male adolescent.

Keith was admitted to the hospital for tests related to abdominal difficulties. He was to be put into a ward with patients his own age. When he arrived, no bed was available in the adolescent ward, so Keith was sent to a ward with younger children, the oldest being eleven. We later learned that Keith did not like this at all, but at the time he said very little. In the evening, the nurse on duty asked Keith if he wanted to play with the younger children. He did not respond, but as the evening progressed he wandered down the corridor to the playroom and began painting a picture. It was a murky picture with a row boat and part of a moon. The very muddy drawing lacks life and vitality. The nurse came by and said how glad she was that Keith had come to the playroom, asking him what he was drawing. Keith did not answer. Then she asked Keith how he was, and again he did not respond. She obviously did not view the drawing as a reliable or valid means of communication. As she continued talking, Keith angrily tore a few pages off the drawing tablet, dipped his brush into the red paint, and wrote the word "UPSET." He threw his paint brush down and returned to bed. The patient had labeled his feelings in firm, large, red printed letters, which the staff could no longer ignore. The young man resorted to the written word for communicating, as writing does convey, to most educated persons, more reliable and valid messages than pictures.

The next day, when I was informed of his behavior, I asked to see the pictures. I discovered that his painting had been drawn so heavily that it produced an impression on the paper underneath.

Fig. 11

If the nurse had understood drawings as a means of communication, she might have seen how murky, how sad, how disillusioned, how " upset" Keith was with his hospitalization, his health, and his life situation. Only when she saw the written word "UPSET" did she comprehend what the drawing communicated and what the patient was trying to express. What might appear to the casual observer to be a tranquil scene is actually not. The pressure of the pencil expressed Keith's suppressed anger and frustration and his need to press through — to get out! Later, I learned that Keith had at last been sent to the adolescent ward.

In a contrasting case, a six year old, still in bed at midday, drew one of the Disney animal characters alone, abandoned, and with tears on its face. Instead of passing this off as "just another drawing," the therapist asked the little girl why there were so many tears on the face of the animal. She replied that he was not good, that he had to be alone, and that no one wanted to play with him. The therapist asked, "What can we do for him?" The child said, "Nothing!" The therapist insisted she could not bear to see this happen and asked the girl to help her discover something they could do for the lonely animal. They decided to draw other animals around and to invite this animal to play with them. Soon this

Disney character was a happy one, enjoying companionship and fun with friends.

Later the therapist learned from the social worker that on the previous day the parents had visited and told their daughter they could not see her until the next weekend because the journey of over a hundred miles was too long to make daily. The child would have to be in the hospital alone for five days. Apparently she had portrayed her own feelings of abandonment in the drawing of the lonely animal. After the visit with the therapist, the child left her bed, sought the company of other children, and was later found playing happily with them in the playroom. Here we find someone accepting a drawing as a valid and reliable means of communication, learning from it, and using it to relieve a stressful situation. The actual drawing was the healing, and brought the child back to a happier state.

Our third premise is an essential consideration in picture interpretation — that mind and body, psyche and soma, are inherently linked. Through this linkage they continually communicate and cooperate. For the purpose of clarity, we speak of the psyche and soma as separate entities, yet they are actually two parts of the totality of the individual. As in a marriage, the psyche and soma work together constantly in a balancing process within the individual.

A prospective element is found to exist in some dreams and drawings — a prospective of either psyche or soma or the combination of both. These elements give insight to future happenings within the internal or external world. Drawings of this nature can thus offer solutions to difficult problems. When working with the seriously ill, such drawings can be useful in helping the patient travel the journey he has begun. However, it is important when working with prospective drawings and dreams to keep in mind Jung's reservations about dreams as prophesies:

> It would be wrong to call them [dreams] prophetic, because at bottom they are no more prophetic than a medical diagnosis or a weather forecast. They are merely an anticipatory combination of probabilities which may coincide with the actual behavior of things but need not necessarily agree in every detail. Only in the latter case can we speak of 'prophecy'" (Jung 1978, CW 8, pg. 255).

Jung's use of the word "forecast" is important for us. We could easily see prospective drawings as giving forecasting information, and wait to see what comes next. My colleagues and I have found increasing evidence of forecasting information in drawings by seriously or terminally ill individuals. Similar to Jung's findings, we find "meaningful" drawings produced during critical phases of life — early youth, puberty, middle-age, and within sight of death.

In the past thirty years, the use of pictures as a reliable and valid tool in psychological assessment has grown in scope. Today we call this area of study and research "projective drawings" or "projective techniques." Some well-known projective tools are listed in *The Clinical Application of Projective Drawings* (Hammer, 1980):

Draw-A-Person-In-The-Rain (Arnold Abrams): Attempts to elicit clues to self-concept under conditions symbolizing environmental stress.

House-Tree-Person, or HTP, (John N. Buck): A technique designed to aid the clinician in obtaining information concerning an individual's sensitivity, maturity, flexibility, efficiency, degree of personality integration, and interaction with the environment, specifically and generally.

Kinetic-Family-Drawing, or KFD, (Robert C. Burns and S. Harvard Kaufman): This technique is about actions, styles, and symbols appearing as primary disturbances in the individual's "family." It was designed for children, particularly troubled children; however, it is an excellent tool for adults as well.

Regressed-Kinetic-Family Drawing, or RKFD, (Furth): A drawing of yourself and your family at age five, making everyone doing something, and avoiding the use of stick figures.

Eight-Card-Redrawing-Test (Leopold Caligor): This probes the deepest layers of the subject's psychosexual identification.

Figure-Drawing (Karen Machover): This technique presents the individual not only with the problem of drawing a person, but with the problem of orienting, adapting, and behaving in a particular situation.

These techniques are used by counselors, therapists, and analysts in aiding a patient's growth. Some professionals believe that assigned topics for the patient to draw are less useful than patient-generated topics. For example, requesting someone to "draw whatever you like" may provide more opportunity for expression than specific intructions to "draw you and your family, making everyone doing something, with no stick figures." I have found that both types of drawings are informative and reach into the individual's unconscious.

When we understand that an individual's inner and outer worlds are interconnected, we can see how the inner situation can be projected onto the outer world and how the outer world affects the inner world. In other words, the conscious and unconscious worlds are intertwined and affect each other, and this relatedness is expressed in pictures to differing degrees.

I began to work with drawings with the premise that only spontaneous drawings could contain unconscious material. As I continued to decipher drawings, I discovered that even pictorial elements and motifs directly suggested by the therapist reveal the patient's unconscious, and thus that spontaneous drawings are not the only method by which the unconscious reveals itself. The unconscious forms its own unique and individual path in which its content manifests itself in the outer world. A trained eye can decipher this presentation and begin to understand the individual path, learning what one's unconscious has to "say" about one's individual psyche.

In this matter, my opinion differs from that of Dr. Jacobi. In her book she describes unconscious drawings as those with "unconscious direction of the choice of the pictorial elements and motifs that are retained" (Jacobi 1969, p.34). She maintains that pictures from the unconscious are valid "so long as these represent spontaneous manifestations of inner process- es or images." Susan Bach (1969) also takes the position that "spontane- ous drawings" reveal unconscious content, omitting the relevance of drawings that have some outside direction. By definition, "spontaneous" means having no external cause or influence. Given these definitions, it seems to me that these two authors deny the interconnectedness of the inner and the outer worlds. The term *impromptu*, however, allows for the outer world to have an influence on the picture as well.

In practical terms, the unconscious seen in light of impromptu work can reveal itself through directed drawings. "Commissioned" paintings and drawings are therefore a valuable tool in revealing aspects of the pa- tient's unconscious. Great artists, as well as lay artists who are asked to draw a specific motif, cannot help revealing a certain amount of their own unconscious content through their art, an assertion we will study more closely in Chapters Four and Six.

As mentioned earlier, it doesn't really matter which drawing proce- dure one follows, since all drawings lead to the individual's psyche or un- conscious content. I have no best drawing method, though I do have favorites, depending upon the patient and what is happening in his or her life at the time. My preference comes from my training, my likes and dislikes, and in no way does it attempt to say that another drawing method does not lead to the individual psyche. In short, "all roads lead to Rome." Most projective techniques provide valid information, and no projective technique outweighs the others. The particular technique used depends on the individual's present situation and on which tool works best for the therapist and the patient. Above all, students need to be assisted in developing their unique selves in the therapeutic process, and only then can they begin to concentrate on learning academic theories.

Students frequently attempt to imitate the work of their teachers. Some try to guess how another professional would do the work. What tends to work for one counselor may not work for another. An ancient Chinese saying cautions that if the wrong person uses the right means, the right means work the wrong way (Jung 1967, CW 13, pg. 7). This stands in sharp contrast to Western beliefs in the "right" method irrespective of the person who applies it. In reality, everything depends on the person and little or nothing on the method.

For instance, I like trees and plants and I am attracted to them in a picture. I am also interested in what characters are doing in a drawing, so I pay particular attention to that as well. By so doing, I can put together possible ideas, questions, and directions in dealing with a patient; on the other hand, some of my colleagues are interested in colors, shapes, and directions of movement. They might concentrate on colors, determining to what extent there are anomalies in their depiction. Eventually they arrive at conclusions about the patient that are similiar to mine, even though we had all started from our personal areas of interest. Following one's own interests ultimately provides the best clues to a therapist. Again, I must rely on Jung's words in order to best express what I mean:

> Practical medicine is and has always been an art, and the same is true of practical analysis. True art is creation, and creation is beyond all theories. That is why I say to any beginner: "Learn your theories as well as you can, but put them aside when you touch the miracle of the living soul. Not theories, but your own creative individuality alone must decide" (Baynes, pg. 361).

CHAPTER 3

COLLECTING DRAWINGS
An Approach and Procedure

The irrational fullness of life has taught me never to
discard anything, even when it goes against all our
theories (so short-lived at best) or otherwise admits
of no immediate explanation. It is of course dis-
quieting, and one is not certain whether the compass
is pointing true or not; but security, certitude, and
peace do not lead to discoveries.
C.G. Jung

To read spontaneous and/or impromptu drawings and to understand their meaning, we must first become aware of the conditions under which the pictures were drawn. This awareness is necessary regardless of the patient's age. The example of a teacher who diagnosed a young boy's emotional state as deeply depressed and severely disturbed — because the child had drawn his entire picture in black — amply illustrates this need for environmental awareness. The teacher, being competent, concerned, and protective of his students, immediately sought counsel from the school psychologist. The psychologist began to probe into the young child's life and his social ties with friends, church, school, and family in an attempt to explain the deep depression. Finally the child was asked directly why he drew his picture in black. He innocently replied that the black crayon was the only one he found in his desk and that he had left his other crayons at home! Not wanting to be reprimanded, he had remained silent about his forgetfulness.

This example shows that the condition — which include the materials at hand, the directions given, lighting, general environment, and all external variables — may have a profound effect on the way pictures look and what they reveal. External factors need to be checked regularly in the gathering of drawings for interpretation.

27

The Initial Approach

My first experience collecting drawings occurred in a hospital ward. I asked all the patients if they would like to draw. Although research for my doctoral dissertation made me particularly interested in the drawings of terminally ill children, it would hardly have been possible to ask only these children to draw. All children on the ward had to be included, invited to draw, given time, and their decision to participate or not had to be respected.

I want to clarify that the approach outlined below is an initial approach that proved successful in my situation. I have found that the general ideas presented here are valid whether the patient is a child or adult, in-patient or out-patient, with a serious or relatively minor physical illness.

Sometimes I begin with the first child I encounter, or I go to the first patient who seems prepared for a visitor. I greet the child as well as any family members present. I tell the patient my name, ask his or her name, and explain that I go about the hospital collecting pictures from all the people who will draw for me.

I do not collect drawings from patients only—especially if a family member is present. I have obtained very informative drawings from siblings and other members of the patient's family. When meeting with an older child or an adult, I explain that I also collect drawings from children and adults in schools, churches, clubs, universities, and other organizations and institutions.

If the child responds positively, I invite him to the area where pencils and paper are supplied for drawing. If the child does not want to draw, I inform him of where I will be located in case he changes his mind. Children seldom refuse an invitation to draw, although a few have declined my offer only to reverse their decision later.

If a patient needs to remain in bed because of apparatus or because of his physical condition, then I give him colored pencils and a board with paper so he can draw in bed. I stay with him while he draws.

When an adult comes to my office I ask him or her to draw at a nearby table in the room where we customarily meet. I always sit with patients while they draw, and I avoid interrupting them in the process. I do keep notes of what they say and ask during the process. I attempt, however, to refrain from responding in order to allow the patient to interact as much as possible with the drawing.

Materials

I have found that a box of standard colored pencils should be used instead of bulky crayons. Pencils allow greater detail. Felt pens should not be used because they do no permit shading and always result in the same intensity of color. A graphite pencil with an eraser should be included.

An eraser is important, especially if the patient asks for one. Observation of what is erased allows for psychological insight to areas of difficulty that the patient is presently encountering and working on.

Standard white typing paper is used since it makes drawing easier. If the paper is too large it is difficult for a child to handle, and if it is too small, a young patient's manual dexterity may not be developed enough to express his or her ideas within such limited space. The patient should be allowed to draw either horizontally or vertically, and the direction or placement of the paper should not be dictated.

It is advisable to have sufficient drawing materials available. If the full range of colors and the preferred paper size are not available, one should continue nevertheless, keeping in mind the limitations of these drawings and making a note of them. Very informative pictures are still obtainable without the use of proper materials: for instance, I have seen drawings made with a ball point pen on the back of an envelope which aided a patient toward a profound change in his life.

In out-patient clinics, the patient may be able to draw while waiting for the doctor, or between preliminary tests and a return visit to the examining room. If this is done, it is very important to remember that once a patient begins to draw, he should definitely be allowed to draw without interruption. The patient should never be hurried by an anxious nurse, aide, doctor, or parent.

For example, if a patient could not finish because a nurse called him in to see the doctor, the picture could be missing many important details. This omission would not be controlled by the patient's unconscious or consciousness. Such omissions represent the imposing external reality of a hurried hospital or an impatient adult, not the inner reality of the patient. A person needs time to draw at his own pace. If the patient is rushed and cannot finish the drawing to his satisfaction, then the therapist should hesitate to evaluate it. It is important to have patience, to give the patient ample time to draw, and to keep instructions short and open-ended.

Outside Assistance

Paralleling the need not to rush the person who is drawing is a very important consideration concerning outside assistance from parents, siblings, nurses, and doctors. I refer here to those who want to add to the patient's picture. The reader may be surprised to find that siblings, however, tend not to interfere with their brother's or sister's drawing nearly as much as do parents, nurses, and doctors. A drawing is a reflection of the patient's psyche; if outsiders begin picking up pencils and drawing on the work, it is no longer an accurate reflection. Others should never be allowed to draw on the patient's private work or to make suggestions about how it should be drawn.

It is a good idea to keep an extra set of pencils with paper on a clipboard easily accessible at all times. This is for the art critic who happens along and begins to tell the artist what to draw, how to draw, where to draw particular objects, what colors to use, and then criticizes the picture. This pseudo-art enthusiast's advice ceases immediately when you remark; "Please, the picture is his (the patient's) and he is doing quite well. I have paper and pencils right here for you to do your own drawing." Follow this comment by handing the extra board to the critic.

Family members often back away, but parents occasionally consent to draw. Once I was amused by a parent who became so involved with her drawing that the patient, having finished, proceeded to nag the mother to hurry because he wanted to leave.

Nurses and doctors should be handled in the same way. If they attempt to draw on the patient's drawing, they should be handed paper and pencils. In most cases they shun the materials and do not interfere again. However, it would be interesting to have the medical staff participate in drawing. It might be quite revealing to see what these professionals are carrying around within themselves.

Verbal Directions

The specific verbal directions for impromptu drawings are simple and short. While handing the patient paper and a complete set of sharpened, colored pencils, I ask him to draw whatever he would like to draw. If the patient says he cannot think of anything to draw, I give him suggestions. For example, in response to "I don't know what to draw," I say, "You could draw your house or your favorite place or maybe you've been somewhere or done something you'd like to draw. Can you tell me about something that has happened to you recently?" If the patient then tells me of some incident, I ask, "What part of that could you draw?"

If the individual is not hurried, he eventually does get started, and often he gets very involved in the drawing as well. It is helpful to "feel" the situation, to be supportive of the person by offering some ideas, but not to overdo it. The patient needs to enter the activity at his own pace. Occasionally the person seems lost or stuck, and then it is prudent to give specific suggestions such as "Can you draw your home or school?" However, one must be careful to allow time for the patient to think for himself after the initial suggestion.

Classifying the Data

When collecting and studying drawings, one must be careful to classify the data in such a way as to ensure an accurate interpretation. On the reverse side of every drawing, I put the date of the drawing and the name and age of the patient. If more than one picture is drawn on this date, I number each picture according to the order in which it is drawn. I also specify the directions given—Impromptu drawing, Draw-A-Tree Drawing, Regressed-Kinetic-Family-Drawing (RKFD), Kinetic-Family-Drawing (KFD), etc., so as to know later on how the subject matter may have evolved.

Usually I do this immediately after the patient gives the picture to me, and then I turn it over and admire it with a very general comment and ask if the patient would like to tell me anything about the picture. I listen very carefully to the comments and, whenever possible, tape-record the story the patient tells. If tape recording is impractical, then I write notes and comments immediately after the patient departs.

If I do not recognize an object or a design, I ask the patient about it. It is not necessary to ask directly, "What is this?", but rather, "Tell me about this object," while pointing to an unrecognizable shape or design. With some patients one may be more general, for instance: "Tell me what is happening in the lower half of your picture," or "Describe in more detail what's happening in the upper left corner of your picture."

I never attempt to ask direct questions that call for "yes" or "no" replies, but approach the patient with open-ended questions and encourage a narrative response with "tell me more." This shows an interest in the drawing, and moreover, an interest in different aspects of the person who did the drawing. The patient should be encouraged to speak in paragraphs, since this allows him to confront psychic energy gathered around symbols presented in drawings. This movement of the psychic energy is accomplished by drawing the symbols and also by talking about them, enhancing them, and building upon them.

Patients draw particular symbols that they select from their world. They use these symbols to share intimate information of their personal selves. Let us now examine some techniques that will help us decipher the valuable messages these drawings contain.

Chapter 4

FOCAL POINTS TO UNDERSTANDING DRAWINGS
Diagnostic and Therapeutic Aids

Follow the argument where it leads.
— *Socrates*

Nowhere in his voluminous writings does Jung outline a systematic approach to deciphering pictures, which is unfortunate, since picture interpretations are similar to dream analyses, though specific links have never been proposed. Susan Bach, as cited earlier, has contributed some guidelines, and Jolande Jacobi wrote an early guidebook to facilitate the task of picture interpretation.

The focal points presented here incorporate the guidelines of Bach and Jacobi, in addition to those of others. I prefer the term "focal point" to "guideline" because it is literally *what* our attention focuses on in the picture that gives us an indication as to how to approach the patient's psyche. Naturally, we must always recognize that no single focal point exclusively determines the status of the psyche; a combination of many focal points and their characteristics needs to be considered. In this book I deal only with drawings; however, the same focal points can also be recognized in clay, collage, photomontage, sculpture, and other forms of art.

After the creators of these drawings completed their work, they had the opportunity to discuss them with me if they so desired. In most cases, little or no comment was made. What statements were made frequently attempted rational explanations and thus had little to do with unconscious content, the more important inner meaning. The same phenome-

32

non appears in dream analysis. The patient wants to explain the dream, but the rational explanation often has little to do with his own unconscious content.

The purpose of this book—and the formulation of focal points for interpreting the illustrations—is to help analysts and therapists become more familiar with diagnostic projective techniques. This is a difficult task because therapists are at different levels of knowledge in this field. Thus, these focal points are broad in scope and designed to facilitate the analytical process by suggesting questions and possible directions to be pursued.

Earlier we discussed how a complex develops and how it may manifest itself externally. We realize that making contact with any aspect of a complex always affects its overall structure. Regardless of what part of the complex is "touched," it and its potency will be altered. With this insight in mind, let us return to pictures.

We know that the content is unconscious and that it activates psychic energy. This energy is of course connected to the complex in some manner. So where do we begin picture work? We know that it matters little where we begin, since all individual complexes are at some level interconnected. We can begin with colors, shapes, sizes, direction of movement, etc.; what matters is that within the drawing the complex is intertwined with all its components in an incredibly intricate pattern. The therapist and patient begin with what is signalled by the symbols. These signals make themselves known through focal points, which draw the therapist's and client's attention. Through focal points, the unconscious directs the healing process.

One of the greatest dangers of projective techniques is the failure to recognize that the work produced is extremely individual. The pictures are subjective creations. Aesthetics, color tone, likes, dislikes, and so forth are all subjective traits that the individual artist will include at his discretion. These elements can be considered in picture analysis; however, evaluation of a picture's psychological content and "feeling" is what will be most informative.

The drawings in this chapter have been collected from the United States, England, Germany, Holland, Switzerland, Finland, Sweden, Canada, and Australia. The drawings are divided into two categories, spontaneous and impromptu, both of which are explained in the Introduction. All of the drawings were executed either free style or on a selected topic. A free style allows the individual to draw whatever is of interest to him. Selected topics can vary, although these topics are usually directed into one of the following categories: a Regressed-Kinetic-Family-Drawing (RKFD), which is a drawing of oneself and one's family at age five, making everyone doing something, and avoiding the use of stick figures; or a present-day Kinetic-Family-Drawing (KFD) of oneself and one's family, showing everyone doing something, and avoiding the use of stick figures. Also included are a few drawings from a variety of categories with specific instructions to individual situations. For example, one is from a patient who was questioning his achievement possibilities. In that case I used the direction to draw oneself picking an apple from an apple tree. There are so many possibilities in what drawings can teach us that I have selected these categories only as a beginning point in understanding and interpreting the nonverbal language of the psyche.

I find this use of nonverbal communication an extremely helpful tool in my specialized work with seriously ill patients, as well as with healthy children and adults. I began to use drawings by healthy individuals to uncover problem areas and to aid in the growth process. The drawings presented here thus illustrate my experience with both ill and healthy patients.

Approach to Picture Interpretation

In first approaching picture interpretation, a person may feel somewhat apprehensive because this is a pioneering method of psychological evaluation, and one is confronted with numerous variables and no set rules. A novice wonders how it is possible to "see" what a picture "says." Hearing with the eyes is a formidable task, but it is, in fact, the person who approaches picture analysis with apprehension who will most probably succeed in it. This person not only fears he does not know: often he knows he does not know, and that in a certain sense is all the better. The picture knows, and one need only "listen" to the picture. In short, there is only one rule for picture interpretation: to know that one does not know. With this in mind, the therapist need only follow three main principles in analyzing unconscious pictures.

The first principle is to always note one's initial impression of a picture. One should not interpret the picture, but rather concentrate on one's initial feeling, (e.g. recall Freud and the Moses statue in Chapter One). It is not necessary to share this impression with the patient; the analyst should become conscious of his own impression, and perhaps even store this information until a later date. For example, if one sees a monster in a picture and the patient sees an angelic figure instead, this can be an indication of how close or far away the therapist is from the patient's actual psychic condition, as well as of who is closest to inner and outer reality. The patient might claim that the devouring dragon (which he perceives as an angel) in the drawing represents his wife. This may not be far from the unconscious truth, so in this case the analyst's impression could be quite accurate and close to the patient's unconscious world. Regardless of what the therapist does, it is crucial that he not fix on a specific decision because of personal associations, but rather allow the patient's associations to develop, and thus for the mystery and ambiguity of his repressed contents to emerge.

The drawing should be approached gradually. In her *Assessing Personality Through Tree Drawings* (1977, pg. 63), Karen Bolander suggests imitating the primitive who "feels into" what he perceives. Sir Laurens van der Post writes of how the Bushman takes hours to stalk his prey, how he moves toward his goal steadily and with no undue haste. A primitive man aligns himself with his goal and establishes a psychic rapport with it. One should establish a similar communication with the drawing. If concrete interpretations come to mind, they should be noted but stored in one's memory bank for later use. Initially one needs to stay with feelings, not interpretations.

The second principle is for the analyst to act as a researcher. The unconscious voice varies from one drawing to another, so its manifestation in each picture should be analyzed objectively. Looking at focal points systematically is the best way for a therapist to order and direct analytic work; and this systematic approach could hinge on a series of objective reactions to the materials and form of a drawing.

First, one must ask about the materials used in the picture. Were they expensive or cheap? Is the paper of good quality or just plain newsprint? Are the materials and paper consistent with each other, or is one of better quality than the other? One must wonder what the answers to these questions mean to the client. Does cheap material devalue his work or express his attitude towards his unconscious? Or could the materials be a compensation of the value of his work?

Second, the size of the paper used should be considered, especially in its relationship to the size of the drawing. If the relationship is off-balance, it could indicate a psychic disturbance in the patient, and the therapist needs to wonder what this lack of relatedness means, that is, why the drawing dwarfs or is dwarfed by the actual paper. From this information, can we wonder about a complementary or compensatory aspect of either introversion or extraversion? Such general observations often give the analyst a valuable initial understanding of what is happening in the patient's psyche. A sometimes equally valuable consideration is how the drawing is laid out on the paper. Horizontal drawings tend to tell a story and vertical drawings tend to make a statement. The therapist needs to observe what his client could be saying by this logistical placement of drawing on paper.

Another fruitful element in the development of the analyst's objective reaction to a picture is the role of its focal points. To mention only a few, a researcher looks at color, shape, direction of movement, placement, number of repeated objects, and missing items. Not all these suggested considerations apply universally to all drawings, so the researcher must break the drawing down into its components, and only then decide the appropriate elements on which to focus.

The third and often most difficult principle in picture interpretation is to synthesize what has been learned from individual components and assemble this information into a whole.

Once the analyst approaches individual pictures with these three interpretive principles in mind, he will find it easier to identify focal points in drawings and what can be learned from them. Focal points are not recipes but are only indicators of a possible way; they point a direction; they provide a focus; they assist. They are simply flexible analytic tools, not rigid guidelines.

Some researchers in the field of projective techniques have isolated specific meanings for symbols, placement on paper, color choice, and other elements. Other writers warn of the dangers involved in the use of these dictionaries. I think it is important not to make definitive statements and interpretations of symbols, placements, and quadrants; yet I find it useful and productive to be aware of these collective definitions or assessments, while retaining a middle-of-the-road attitude. The analyst should not rely exclusively on symbolic interpretations derived from a dictionary of symbols, nor go to the opposite extreme and completely devalue this approach. My goal in this book is to balance the two approaches.

Focal points are described and presented here as suggestions and aids to deciphering unconscious content as revealed in pictures. Illustrations follow each focal point. Through their use, we as therapists can come closer to comprehending and deciphering pictures diagnostically. Individuals who are entirely unfamiliar with picture analysis can begin to understand the makeup of the unconscious presented in the picture by studying these focal points. These are basic and by no means conclusive. It is important to remember that no one focal point provides conclusive evidence of what is within a patient's psyche, and that a series of drawings is a much more reliable indicator of a patient's psychological and somatic condition, since a given drawing most often expresses psychic activity at the point in time in which it was drawn.

The task of ordering focal points into a sequence is difficult, and no set formula or methodology exists for accomplishing it. The therapist and the patient together need to first determine the focal point's "pull," its internal "energy," and begin analytic work from there. For the sake of clarity, I placed the focal point, "What Feeling Does The Picture Convey," at the beginning of the series—because this particular focal point is useful in allowing the therapist to develop a feel for the drawing before being influenced by the patient's reactions. I listed the "color" focal point last because of its lengthy presentation. I sequenced the remaining focal points in what I feel is to be the order of their relative importance in the development of a picture interpretation. I am open to other ordering systems and to further focal points being added to the list. This is only a suggested beginning.

The last statement that I offer to the reader before journeying through the focal points is an important quote from Jung in reference to the analysis of dream paintings:

> The truth is, we are here moving in absolutely new territory, and a ripening of experience is the first requisite. For very important reasons I am anxious to avoid hasty conclusions. We are dealing with a process of psychic life outside consciousness, and our observation of it is indirect. As yet we do not know to what depths our vision will plumb. (Jung, 1976 *CW* 16, pg. 51).

The fact that we are indeed exploring uncharted territory must be kept in mind as we begin our analysis of the focal points in unconscious pictures.

WHAT FEELING DOES THE PICTURE CONVEY?

A picture or drawing always communicates a feeling. It is important to capture the initial, spontaneous impression first, and if possible, to encapsulate it in one word—such as "happy," "sad," "frustrated," "fearful," "confined"—rather than evaluating the picture concretely. The individual can also be asked how he felt while drawing the picture or what feeling he gets when he looks at the picture. If one finds a conflict between one's own and the patient's impression, one must not transfer one's reactions to the patient, but rather delve into the nature of his experiences with his picture. Through this process of examining differing or various reactions, the therapist may reach a fuller understanding of the patient's feelings.

Agony, horror, fear, are the feelings evoked by this spontaneous drawing. Cathy, age sixteen, drew this picture six months after her father's death. She had been extremely close to her father and since his death had run away from home many times. She says that no one likes her, and views her father's death as a black time in her life. She perceives him as the only person who understood her.

Fig. 12

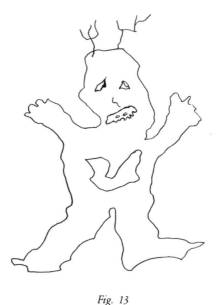

Fig. 13

Fright, fear, terror are the feelings conveyed by Emmie's impromptu drawing. She is fourteen, pregnant, and living in the custody of the courts because her mother is unfit to care for her and her father has sexually abused her. Although she is determined to have an abortion within a few days, she is terrified of her mother's reaction to this decision. She is equally fearful of the responsibility inherent in raising and supporting a child alone. Her counselor said that she is fearful of being reprimanded for having a child at her age, and she is fearful of taking care of a baby." Emmie directly communicates her feelings of fear in this drawing.

Joy, gaiety, happiness jump out of the following drawing. For Helen, fifty-seven, Christmas obviously holds a great deal of meaning. In discussing her drawing, she emphasizes that the holiday season is celebrated in her family to the fullest, not only for one day, but for several weeks. The tone this spontaneous picture is festive and exciting.

Fig. 14

WHAT IS ODD?

A helpful guideline in picture interpretation is to try to discover why some things are drawn in a peculiar fashion, or abnormally. For example, a clock with letters instead of numbers, a car flying in the sky, a person with three hands, or a dog with five legs. This odd representation often points out a specific problem area of which the individual may or may not be aware but which needs to be brought into the open.

Fig. 15

This RKFD was done by Marilyn, age thirty. It is from a memory of herself at age five. Several elements are odd in this picture. The mother's shadow is not in alignment with her feet, the sun on the far left edge is very small and incomplete, and Marilyn does not have any legs or feet. Most significant and noticeable of all is the penis-pitch-fork her father uses in the hay. This woman revealed the anxiety she had over sexual intercourse, feeling fearful of the male organ and vulnerable. Although her father never molested her, another man in the community did. She remembered her father towel drying her at age four and the look he had in his eyes as he dried her genital area. Around the farm she always dreaded seeing her father's eyes, as they often had that look in them. She grew up in fear of what he could do to her.

In this RKFD by Alice, age thirty, the paths to the neighbors' houses do not lead to their doors. This is very odd. Upon further investigations we discovered Alice had cancer and received no support from neighbors, friends, or relatives. "They don't want to talk about my having cancer and they don't want me to bring it up either." The paths being oddly drawn show her lack of accessibility to neighbors, friends, and relatives.

Fig. 16

It is also odd to see trees growing in sidewalk paths. Alice said: "Yes, I do find I put up barriers in my life to block myself from completing the things I have begun. And at the same time I have an excuse, because the tree is in my way. I can't continue on my journey. I wonder now if having cancer is the 'ultimate tree'." Upon last report, Alice was doing fine physically.

This drawing is by Lowry, age eighty-nine. A renowned British artist, he died in 1976. At an exhibition of his drawings I noted how odd it was to see in this drawing the inward fold of the man's coat in the chest area. The coat should be falling downward, pulled by gravity, but instead it goes inward. While viewing his other work, I noted this odd detail did not appear. He had shown proper folding of clothing elsewhere. Knowing that he died a few months before this exhibition I wondered if this picture, dated the year before his death, could reveal through this detail physical problem in that area of his body, the heart region. Later I found Lowry's death certificate in the exhibition hall records. It stated the primary cause of death: heart failure.*

The author thanks the London Royal Academy of Arts for permission to use this drawing.

Fig. 17

BARRIERS

Note where barriers are within a picture. A barrier can be a person, plant, tree, or an inanimate object such as a wall, car, chair, or door. One can see who is blocking whom from communicating, or perhaps begin to discover other barriers, conscious or unconscious, which may exist between the individuals depicted in the drawing.

This KFD was drawn by Marie, age thirty-five. The man she lives with is reading the blueprints of the dream house they want to build. She draws herself carrying a building block to the front wall of the house. Her son is to the far right playing by himself. She noticed two important factors in the drawing: the building of this dream house is becoming a barrier to her relationship with her son, and she does all the work to build this dream house. Both factors are true in her life. Notice also that the table

Fig. 18

and blueprints are barriers to the man's genital area. Marie reported that their sexual activities have almost ceased, and the man has announced to her that he is bisexual and having other relationships.

Fig. 19

In this RKFD, we see Michelle contained inside the front window. Michelle is now fifty-two years old. The house is a barrier between her and her family members, and is a symbol of all the norms her father expected her to live up to. She especially wanted a closer connection to him, but in his free time away from work he maintained the car and had no time for her. The car and house are barriers to Michelle and her father making contact.

We see mother pushing the carriage. The carriage and the baby, in turn, are barriers between Michelle and her mother. In reality this was true. Michelle reported, "Once it happened that I was pushing the carriage and by 'accident' it upended and the baby fell out. I ran away and hid out of fear. Neighbors told my mother of my whereabouts. I was afraid." Five-year-old Michelle wanted to be the baby in the carriage and to feel the physical warmth her mother was giving to the baby. She wanted a home which she felt was not there for her anymore.

We see a variety of subtle barriers such as walls, furniture, and other objects in this KFD by Frank, age nineteen. In addition, everyone is privately occupied in his or her own compartments. One wonders whether,

Fig. 20

with each individual separated physically, their emotions are stifled and closed off as well. The parents are divorced. His sister is married and has moved out of the home, and Frank is still having difficulty relating to her. Frank lives with his mother and they have many problems communicating.

WHAT IS MISSING?

Observe what is absent or left out of the picture. The missing elements may be quite significant to the individual . What they represent or symbolize could possibly be absent from the person's life.

In this RKFD, Catherine, thirty-five, draws all family members engaged in their own activities. Father is at work as a police officer, brother is drawing on an easel, mother is holding younger sister and Catherine is pushing the baby buggy. It is interesting to note that mother is the only individual missing feet and hands. Catherine reported, "Mother couldn't stand on her own two feet. When I was a child, mother was a very dependent woman. She never stood up to my father for herself. She didn't even know how to write a check or drive a car. But after his death, she became very

Fig. 21

independent at age fifty. She remarried five years later and returned to her old mold of the dependent woman."

In this picture we understand how the person drawing omits hands and feet on the mother. The mother was perceived as not really using them.

Dorothy, fifty-two, draws a family picnic in this KFD. People are doing a variety of activities— building a fire, playing with a ball, and preparing food. When asked where the father is, the response was, "He is in the boat." However, we do not see anyone in the boat. Then father is not

Fig. 22

on this page; he is missing. Missing individuals are often a sign of conflict. In this case, her father had beaten Dorothy at age seven so badly that her hearing was severely impaired. He had also threatened the life of her mother and was seen as violent, verbally as well as physically.

Fig. 23

This impromptu picture—with sky, earth, flowers, two trees, and a house—was drawn by Teresa, age six. The door is missing from the house. Teresa suffered from leukemia. She was a very introverted child and at times difficult to communicate with. A door allows accessibility, but in many ways Teresa was inaccessible and would only express herself through gestures and nonverbal signs, although it was physically possible for her to have spoken had she so chosen.

WHAT IS CENTRAL?

Often what is drawn in the center of the picture may indicate where the core of the problem lies or what is important to the individual.

Fig. 24

Mary, forty-two, drew her husband centrally positioned, carrying a sixty-pound can of honey in this KFD. He has just finished helping his wife fill a bowl of honey, the red jar on the counter. Mary says, "His arms are in a position of carrying a baby and I did not want to leave them empty; so I put the can of honey in his arms." It turned out that ten years earlier Mary became pregnant and her husband had decided she should abort. She argued with him, but he insisted. Finally, when she was at the doctor's office for the abortion, she told her husband that she wouldn't go through with it since she felt it was the wrong thing for her to do. He insisted and she capitulated out of fear. Mary's central issue today is with her husband's refusal to accept responsibility for the abortion. She feels the pain of this loss and he seems not to suffer from it at all. If only she knew he also suffered the loss of this unborn child, she would not feel so alone.

We see her standing over her husband waving her hand, perhaps indicating a goodby or a need for gaining attention. We discussed this, and Mary said that if she left her husband and the four children, he would finally feel a sense of loss and then he would be able to relate to her loss of the aborted child.

Fig. 25

This impromptu drawing by Darlene, sixteen, shows a tree with a large scar on the trunk. The scar is central in the picture. Scars frequently indicate a trauma in the individual's life. We know that Darlene has been rejected by her mother and that she is an abused child, physically and emotionally; yet she desperately wants to return to her mother. This is the only kind of love she knows thus far and she does not want to lose it, always hoping the situation will improve.

The tree also symbolizes the feminine, the nourishing, sheltering, protecting, supportive aspects of the Great Mother. Here Darlene has used a compensatory symbol to point out the need she feels for mother love.

SIZE

The proportion of objects and people in a drawing is important. If things are out of proportion, we try to discover what the excessively large figures emphasize and what the excessively small figures appear to devalue.

We immediately notice the large head over the individuals sitting at the dining table in this KFD by George, age twenty-eight. This is the face of the deceased father who still has power over George and the

Fig. 26

family. The dead father's power is enormous, as represented by his oversized head. George wrote: "The picture is dominated by the spirit of my dead father."

In this KFD, Joan, forty-six drew herself and her husband under one umbrella and their children under another. She told me that "the family is on a walk", and I immediately noticed that the individuals are too large to fit through the doorway of their house. I also saw that the children

Fig. 27

appear to be about ten years of age or younger, though I knew that Joan's children were then in their twenties. At this time Joan's home was in a turmoil over the tragic death of one son (black box in right foreground) and consequently the grown children are being watched and mothered by the "Great Mother archetype" inside Joan. She did not see her children as grown, able to care for themselves, and therefore drew them as younger.

Fig. 28

We see an enormous head with very small limbs in this impromptu drawing by Teresa, age six. Following this drawing, Teresa, who was suffering from leukemia, had such severe aches and pains in her limbs that she was hospitalized and could no longer use her extremities. Teresa related to the world with her head and was bedridden until her death. (See case studies, Chapter Six.)

SHAPE DISTORTION

Often some part of a figure or object may be drawn out of proportion. This may symbolically represent problem areas where more concentration and understanding could help return the distortion to normality.

Fig. 29

The shape distortion in Paul's impromptu drawing reveals his somatic condition. Paul, seven, had previously drawn several people with all their parts integrated and connecting. One day while at the hospital for a check-up he drew this distorted character. I talked with the doctor and she reported that Paul had been suffering from severe abdominal pains and earaches. Note the size of the ears and separation of the abdominal region.

Six year-old Arnie distorted the hat of Santa Claus, transforming it into a phallic shape. He referred to the black circular figure with black radial markings at the end of the cap as "Santa's fuzzy," explaining that he didn't have white to make the "ball on the end of the cap." In fact, Arnie not only did have a white pencil, but used it for shading a layer of snow along the entire horizontal surface of the green grass. (Unfortunately, this feature can only be detected on the original drawing, and then only by tilting the paper under a bright light at an angle to reflect and contrast the

Fig. 30

white pencil shading from the white paper).

During the period when this drawing was made, Arnie was under medical care. One of his problems was the presence of red blood cells in his urine. To monitor this problem a nurse was regularly collecting "clean catch" urine specimens that involved cleansing the end of the penis with a cotton ball. This was a very embarrassing experience for Arnie, who was extremely shy. The distorted hat (as well as the black ball on the end) reflect this child's anxiety and obsession regarding a clinical experience he found emotionally traumatic. (The reader is advised to consider the section on "Colors Out of Place." Arnie's father had a short, black beard that may not make the black-bearded Santa as significant as the black ball on the cap. Recall that Arnie indicated that the ball should have been white).*

*The author thanks Yvonne Williams of the Wellspring Counseling and Consulting Resources [Indianapolis] for this drawing and its analysis.

REPEATED OBJECTS

Objects are often repeated in drawings. When this occurs it is usually helpful to count them. The number of objects is frequently quite significant, relating to units of time or events of importance in the past, present, or future.

Fig. 31

In this RKFD by Patty, thirty-two, her brother and mother are in the house while Patty and her father ride horses and work outside on the ranch. The brother could not participate because he was confined to a wheelchair. Notice that the two horses have only six legs. Two legs on the father's horse are missing. Patty tells me she and her father were so close that it seemed they were "riding together." Yet she found as the years passed he depended on her to carry more and more responsibility for the ranch. "It became a burden," she said.

In this impromptu drawing by Ona, age forty-two, we see a footprint covering a major portion of the picture, with flowers all around. On the right toe of the footprint we see a fairy and ant. (In folklore, ants are fairies in their last stage of earthly existence). The picture was drawn with flowers which might, at first glance, seem to be indiscriminately placed upon the page. When counting the flowers, we find thirty-nine clover flowers outside and nine flowers inside the footprint. Ona had a very traumatic affair at age thirty-nine. She adds that she has never experienced

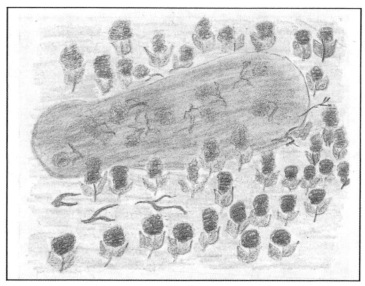

Fig. 32

a sexual relationship that was not destructive, and that there have been nine significant men in her life.

Fig. 33

This impromptu drawing was done by Teresa when she was six. The symmetry in the picture is striking, and one immediately notices the rows of flowers. When we count them, we find ten flowers on the ground and two more in the hands of the little girl. Exactly twelve weeks after she made this drawing, Teresa died. (Geigy, 1969) Susan Bach has shown that drawings by seriously ill patients can reveal that individuals appear to know, at an unconscious level, when their life will end. This is evidenced by pictorial expressions where the number of revealed objects corresponds with a unit of time related to their death.

PERSPECTIVE

Observe the perspective from which the drawing is done. Is the perspective consistent? Different perspectives in the same drawing may indicate inconsistencies that may relate to inconsistencies within the individual's life.

A drawing which is *grossly* out of perspective might be looked at for psychosis. This is sometimes a direct link with the unconscious.

Fig. 34

We see a confusion of perspective in this impromptu drawing by Rosemarie, thirty-three. The lake is seen from above, as if from an airplane, and yet the house on the bottom of the page is seen from the ground or eye level. These are two impossible perspectives to achieve at one time. We should ask, What is confusing about Rosemarie's perspective? She said the purpose of this drawing was to show she had direction. However, Rosemarie, in the boat, has only one oar in hand; the other oar appears as if in her other hand, but is outside the boat. We can see in the drawing that she lacked direction and did not know where she wanted to go. She was seeking a better perspective and possibilities for her professional life.

Fig. 35

Miguel, eleven, did this spontaneous drawing from two perspectives. We see a hockey court from above and from a second perspective — viewing two hockey players from the sideline. The individual is confused or bewildered and most likely inconsistent in his feelings and behavior.

Miguel displayed confusion of family dynamics. His father was in jail for sexual abuse of a cousin. His mother and siblings lived in physical fear of the father and dreaded his release from prison. The great conflict for Miguel was loving *and* fearing his father.

CARRY YOURSELF INTO THE PICTURE

The therapist should attempt to *become* particular objects within the picture in order to feel, hear, and see how they behave, and to better understand their relationship to the whole picture.

This impromptu drawing from Gina, twenty-eight, is of her dream castle and her Prince Charming. We see them in the upper right of the castle; above is a rainbow. A river flows diagonally across the page and flowers bloom below. Gina stated she wanted to find a man, her Prince Charming in life.

When carrying oneself into this drawing to become the Prince Charm-

Fig. 36

ing, one feels as if the Prince Charming is in a very tenuous position. It seems unsafe. Becoming the Prince Charming might make one feel threatened by being pushed off the edge of the palace. This very likely would be a position that a man would not want to get into in his relationship with a woman, as she would be so threatening and overpowering.

Fig. 37

In figure 37, a spontaneous drawing by Janice, thirty-eight, we see two boats. Becoming the boats, I realize that as the large boat I would be pulling a smaller boat that has its sails unfurled. This could be to my disadvantage. And if I am the smaller boat, I have the use of my sails and do not need the larger boat to pull me along. Janice wrote that "I am capable of being much more independent of husband and family than I allow myself to be."

Fig. 38

This spontaneous drawing by thirty year old Yula certainly projects darkness and storm. We find the sunshine covered by dark clouds and stormy weather; however, in this unfriendly atmosphere, the boat with sails up looks calm. The water line is higher on the right side of the boat than on the left side and the difference in water level is dangerous to the boat. We can feel this disequilibrium by carrying ourselves into the picture, and we understand that this could be what is pulling Yula apart. Yula is torn between staying with her father during his dying time and taking care of family responsibilities. Her personal feelings are dark, as we can easily ascertain.

SHADING

More time and energy are invested into objects or shapes that are shaded than in objects or shapes drawn without shading. Energy invested in shading may reflect fixation on, or anxiety about, what the shaded object or shape represents symbolically.

This tree drawing by Mindy, forty, represents her "tree of life." We see the shading along the right side of the tree and lower section of foliage. Mindy was insecure in her life situation and wanted to make sure she had something to hold onto. She was afraid of losing control over her life, afraid to relinquish possible sources of nurturance, even though it appears that her life is strong, healthy, and harmonious. If we look closely, the top of the tree trunk looks like a hand grasping the foliage.

Fig. 39

Six-year-old Danny drew this picture of himself while hospitalized for stabilization of childhood diabetes. In addition to this diagnosis, Danny had serious psychological problems for which he was receiving regular therapy.

Danny is a fair-skinned Caucasian, but he shaded his body with pencil, projecting his anxiety and depression.

Fig. 40

EDGING

A drawing that includes edging consists of a figure or object along the edge of the paper that often even goes off the paper, so that it is only

Fig. 41

partially drawn in the picture. Edging is like "hedging." It is a method of getting involved partially but not being fully committed. It is a way of being present and yet remaining on the outer limits.

This spontaneous drawing by a seventy-two-year-old dying woman is edged to the right of the drawing sheet. She has no physical energy to live, and psychologically she is trying to prepare for movement out of life. She is neither in life nor out of life, she is on the edge and this is the factor that depresses her gravely. She is open to death, but not to the pain she is suffering. She seeks to understand why she cannot die and why she must endure her pain.

Fig. 42

The high school and administration building are edged in this spontaneous drawing by Reggie, sixteen. The residence hall is central in the drawing. Reggie has many problems in school and feels the school places unnecessary restrictions on the students. He does not have the freedom he has at home, and is not committed to his school situation. He understands and admits he is testing his teachers and the administrators.

Fig. 43

Jimmy, twenty-six, travels as an international buyer for a large European firm. In this impromptu drawing we see his home is edged. When I asked about this, he replied that he had no home life and was very lonely. Jimmy attempted to keep homes in a variety of countries, but none worked out for him. He realizes his instability and is searching for a home life with a woman on a steady basis.

COMPARE TO THE SURROUNDING WORLD

A drawing needs to be compared with the state of the actual physical world above and beyond what is represented in the picture. This includes country, culture, race, religion, and season of year. What may be odd or peculiar in one's own world may not be so odd in the world of someone in another culture. However, when we find differences between what is in one's surrounding world and what is shown in a drawing, the difference may be significant in the patient's psychology.

This impromptu drawing by Lois, thirty-eight, shows an apple tree on the right side of the picture with two people and animals at play. This was Lois's favorite tree in her garden. One might wonder about green apples, and why they are not red, but these are Gravenstein apples, which are green. Lois happens to live in an area where that is the major variety produced.

Fig. 44

Fig. 45

Mona, forty-three, draws a pine tree at the side of her house, outside her bedroom window in this spontaneous drawing. When comparing this spontaneous drawing with the actual pine tree, we find one cannot see the base of the real tree because a rather large doghouse is build there. In asking Mona about this she said:

From earliest memory I seemed to be in the doghouse for doing things which upset other people. In the first grade I was unable to keep still unless I concentrated on not talking, and was frequently kept after school because I forgot and talked out of turn. I was always being warned by my mother that I did things without thinking and this would make people upset with me. Even in graduate school I was criticized for operating intuitively instead of following the then accepted 'Body of Knowledge' criteria. I went through life this way until about ten years ago when I joined forces with two friends. We pooled our resources, our energy, and our love and learned to probe our feelings together. I began to spend less time in the doghouse.

However, the doghouse days are still sore spots in Mona's memory.

OUT OF SEASON
Where we see a picture of Christmas trees drawn in July, or an Easter drawing in November, we wonder about the need to have that season early, or what happened during that season which needs to be repeated at this time. Drawings are usually appropriate to the season and should be questioned if they are not.

Fig. 46

This KFD by Katie, age fifty-three, drawn in July, represents an out-of-season picture. I asked myself, "Why a Christmas tree in July?" Was Katie rushing the year, or trying to hold it back? I discovered that Christmas was a very important event in Katie's life. She told me, "It is the biggest, givingest, happiest, lovingest time." Sharing this season with her three children and husband is important, but this year was a very frightening and fearful event in her life. For the first time, her two sons would not be home for Christmas. These two sons were grown and now on their own. Even though it was July, anxiety and fear were already building in Katie for this coming event, and she was preparing in advance for the trauma she was going to feel.

Fig. 47

A mother drew "Welcome to The Christmas Place" as an impromptu drawing in June. She had a ten-year-old son who was not expected to live to see the next Christmas. Her desire to rush and welcome him into the Christmas season, the symbolic time of new birth of life, may have been activated by his precarious life situation.

ENCAPSULATION

Encapsulation implies enclosure, the need to draw specific boundaries around oneself, to set oneself aside or apart from others. Since the individual encapsulated is in a protective covering, one questions what he fears, for what reason must he be enclosed, or what is happening around him that encloses him.

This RKFD is by Carol, age thirty-eight. Her sister, ten years older, is using the jump rope to encapsulate herself. Carol said her sister always seemed off by herself and no one could make contact with her. Likewise, her brother was in a seminary from age twelve and seldom at home. We see he is also encapsulated by work, and mother, often ill, is frequently encapsulated by her bed. Father is encapsulated within the house. As a five-year-old, Carol lies in the sun's rays, alone, separated from all family

Fig. 48

members, trying to "soak up" what warmth she can get. Unfortunately, even the remaining brother performs a lonely activity. There is little, if any, interrelatedness in this RKFD.

This impromptu drawing made by Ralph, age twenty, shows how cut off he is from communication. He is encapsulated in an enclosure in his wheelchair. He feels very far away from others.

Fig. 49

EXTENSIONS

An extension is any device drawn in the hand of a figure. This addition or extra part could be a spoon, a cane or crutch, golf club or baseball bat — anything that allows the individual to exert greater control over his environment. This extension implies either that the person sees himself as having control or that he desires more control (complementary-compensatory), and in this effort he may be either successful or unsuccessful.

Fig. 50

In this KFD we see Keith, age nine, playing miniature golf with his family. Although he pictures himself cheering his mother as she sinks her ball into the hole, it is important to notice that his golf club is almost hitting the head of his younger brother. This club, longer than the other clubs, could easily represent Keith's desire to have control over his family situation, especially over his brother, of whom he was quite jealous at the time.

In the following KFD, Eloise, forty-two, holds a rake in her hands. As an extension this could imply she is reaching out for more control and order. Her personal history indicates she has difficulty in keeping her office in order although she has worked there for seven years. She feels that her emotions are too controlled, and she is unable to release them. The rake, like a comb, is an implement which both gathers things together and

Fig. 51

at the same time smooths and loosens—thus with this extension, she is expressing her need to deal with both her outside office work and her inner feelings and emotions.

BACK OF DRAWING

When the reverse side of the sheet of paper is used for drawing, the therapist should take note of who or what is placed on the back, as this may be indicative of conflict. Why can the person or object not be on the front with the rest of the drawing?

Fig. 52

In this spontaneous drawing by Sue, four and a half, we see mother, brother, friend, and self. They all are "playing together." On the reverse side we see "daddy." The case history shows father is not married to Sue's mother and is not the father of her brother. He visited on weekends until Sue was four, but six months ago he had stopped visiting her, even though he continued to live in the same building. The mother reported that this was difficult for Sue, knowing her father was so close yet so far away. With this information it is understandable that father is drawn on the back of the drawing. Sue is having conflict and difficulty in relating to him. (Note: The therapist wrote the family names on the drawing sheet for the child).

Fig. 52 a

Below we see a spontaneous drawing by Jean, age nine. Jean has placed all five siblings and herself in the drawing. Everyone is busy with something to do and Jean is off for a walk with her teddy bear, asking a brother if he wants to come along. This is typical of Jean, a very loving, sharing child.

Fig. 53

On the reverse side we find mother sleeping on the couch, which has a lamp at the end of it on the far left, and dad watching television. The children seldom had the opportunity to spend time with their parents, and Jean frequently wanted to play with them. She realized at an early age they were uninterested or always too busy, and she went off by herself to discover the world. Jean is in conflict about this and is angry, but she cannot change the situation. Once again, it is understandable that the parents are on the reverse side.

Fig. 53a

UNDERLINING

A figure underscored usually indicates lack of grounding (complementary). However, if one individual in a drawing is not underscored and all other figures are underscored, the individual without underscoring is the steady one (compensation). It is important to keep Jung's theory of compensation in mind as we examine this focal point.

Shirley, age forty, drew the next RKFD. At age five, Shirley saw her father as not being grounded in real life. He was remote and always preoccupied, too afraid of his powerful wife to protect Shirley or to claim her. Shirley wrote, "I had to give him grounding and stability. I needed him to have it for my sake."

In this picture the underlining is complementary.

Fig. 54

In this RKFD, we see May pushing her toy pram under her mother, who is also pushing a pram. Every person is underscored in this drawing except May. Even at the early age of five, May recalls her mother saying to her, "You are the rock in the family." Within the family, May felt that she had to be steadfast and protect all family members. We see in this picture that the underlining is compensatory.

Fig. 55

ERASURES

Note erasures and compare the redrawn work with them. Erasures frequently indicate conflict material or reworked areas of what the symbol represents in life. If the erasure has been redrawn in an improved representation, then this is most likely true in the individual's life. On the contrary, if the erased and redrawn material deteriorated, then the represented material has deteriorated as well. If erased and not redrawn, the individual may still be in conflict about the represented material.

Fig. 56

In Fran's spontaneous drawing, we find a confused fifteen-year-old attempting to gain a better stance and place in her life. Fran is very well developed physically, with nineteen and twenty-year-old men attempting to date her. She also is aware that her parents' relationship is very bad and she is involved in this.

Fran, her boyfriend (of only one week) Brud, and two companions are walking from the boardwalk toward the ocean. She says that the picture is a sunset, but in reality she is facing east, so it would be a sunrise. (We know she is facing east because Fran tells me that she is looking at the Atlantic Ocean from her home town on the East Coast).

We see that Fran erased herself and had difficulty positioning herself in this drawing. She was trying to gain a better placement next to Brud. She was having a sexual relationship with Brud and was trying to get it in order. He left a few days later for the army. This picture was done within a ten-day period before Fran threatened suicide. Her position in life was not solid or clear.

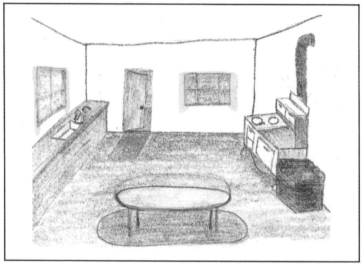

Fig. 57

In this impromptu drawing by Lynn, age thirty-two, we see the kitchen from her childhood home in a remote location. Lynn reported that in her attempt to draw the table she realized that it was not in the correct perspective. She consequently erased it, and the second attempt was much improved. The table had been used by her mother to prepare meals and for preserving foods for the winter months; the table represented the "bread of life" (mother).

Lynn has recently clarified her own role as provider and mother. That is, her nurturing role and its clarification had been worked on in analysis and in the drawing, erasing and redrawing.

On the following page is a spontaneous drawing from Ian, age eleven, we see several erasures of the soldiers' legs. Most notable is the man in a prone position above Ian's name. Ian is seeing a child therapist because he is "bucking" his parents and is trying to find his own stance and grounding in life. He is being stubborn and obstinate in this struggle with his parents, and in this drawing the erasures reflect his search.

Fig. 58

WORDS IN DRAWINGS

Words used in drawings need special attention. The patient who did the drawing fears he or she may not have clearly conveyed the point or message of the drawing, so words add definition to the statement, and thus reduce the drawing's chances of being misinterpreted. Of course we question what has been misinterpreted, and/or what presently is being misinterpreted in the patient's life. The whole issue of trust comes forth when words appear in drawings. It is also a question of how much the patient trusts non-verbal communication.

Fig. 59

In this KFD drawn by Barbara, twenty-eight, we see words used to emphasize a message. Much is going on around this woman in her daily life: "psychology, Sunday-school, learning, teaching, working." She is connected to the home and to all family members by drawn lines. It is no wonder she said, "Sometimes all of this is too much for me. People expect so much from me." Can she trust herself to do what is expected of her? And can she trust that others know she is doing so much? Could it be that she expects too much of herself—psychology, teaching, Sunday-school, learning and working? Words are important in drawings because they make definite points. Barbara wants to make sure we understand she is doing five jobs and that "it is too much."

Fig. 60

This is a spontaneous drawing by Charlotte Salomon, a young Jewish refugee who died in the Holocaust. In her pictorial autobiography, words in her drawings are sometimes an important part of her artistic expression. At other times she creates incredible scenes where words are not needed to convey her message; the drawing does it all.

In the above picture we see an elderly woman whose face shows distress, while an elderly man, perhaps her spouse, is comforting and caring. The words included in this picture read:

> Grandmother: "Oh dear, what times we live in — will I ever see her again?"
> Grandfather: "Don't upset yourself, it won't help matters. I believe in Providence — and what is to be, will be."

Two elders who are close seem concerned and in discussion. In this particular drawing the words seem to me to be an addition to what the picture already communicates nonverbally. What need did she have to say again in words what she has shown so well in the picture?*

*The author thanks the Charlotte Solomon Foundation, Amsterdam, for permission to use this drawing.

LINE ACROSS THE TOP OF A PAGE

A line across the top of a page, such as the sky or just a drawn line, could indicate " something" psychologically overhead. This " something" is frequently a burden to the patient and the patient is fearful of carrying this burden. The fear arises over the need to control this burden or the feeling that control may not be possible.

Fig. 61

This impromptu drawing by Teresa, age six, shows a blue sky lining the top. This young girl is being treated in the hospital for leukemia. She has illustrated through this line at the top the fear she feels about both her treatment and the severity of her disease (See Case Studies, Chapter Six).

Fig. 62

After Karen, age thirty-four, drew this KFD, she said that the line along the top signified "that we are all together, under one roof." Karen wishes to see the situation thus; in reality, however, Karen's marital relationship is not ideal and she is frightened and afraid when faced with the possibility of a family breakup, for separation is a most painful idea to her.

Fig. 63

This spontaneous drawing by Agnes, age fifty-eight, shows a blue sky spanning the top of the picture, indicating a sense of foreboding hanging over an otherwise positive scene. Agnes and her ex-husband were divorced and had not lived together for three years. However, he has recently moved back into her home, and the resulting situation is quite clear. Agnes pulls her wagon, her husband does not pull his. Now, as she senses they must again separate, she is filled with worry and fear about how this will affect their children.

TRANSPARENCY

Transparency is seeing through some barrier to something within, e.g., a transparent wall where you can see the bedroom environment. In young children this is normal. In adolescents or adults, transparency may appear with limited frequency and intensity. However, when one sees the frequency of transparency increasing (i.e., seeing through a wall, then through a person, then through clothing, then through skin to the bone structure) and this accompanies the intensity of seeing into a taboo area (e.g., of sexuality), we have both frequency and intensity at a more developed level. This may be a problem of reality orientation, and a situation of denial could exist.

Fig. 64

In this KFD, Patti, age forty-two, draws herself, her husband and two children. The outer wall on their house is transparent and Patti tells me this transparent wall on the house means to her "that things are going through (her). They don't stick in (her)." Patti has difficulty being aware of what goes on around her in the family dynamics.

MOVEMENT

Trajectory

The therapist should follow the trajectory of moveable objects, weapons, and people, note their direction, and determine what the consequences will be.

In abstract drawings it is informative to note movement and flow of the color and/or design, to see how they may overflow and what they may move toward within the drawing.

Fig. 65

In this KFD by Ruth, age thirty-eight, we have splendid illustrations of trajectory. We see both sons with arm extensions and between them their sister riding a horse. If the son with the baseball bat extended his arm, he could reach his sister and the horse as well. On the other hand, the daughter could easily ride her horse directly over this brother. Ruth reported, "There is a love-hate relationship between my son and daughter."

Similarly, the son with the tennis racket could swing it against his sister's horse. The horse would then take off, running over his younger brother. When asked, Ruth commented: "There definitely is competition between these two boys."

Fig. 66

In this KFD, Kenneth, age thirty-seven, depicts many activities. If we center on the trajectory of the arrow in the hands of the figure in the lower right corner, we find it is aimed at Kenneth's sister on the left side of the coconut tree. He wrote: "My sister was born at home when I was seventeen. Everybody was away except me and the midwife. I felt very involved with the birth. When my sister was three, I wanted to take her away because I felt my parents were doing a bad job of bringing her up. I wanted to take control of rearing her. I did not want them to repeat the bad job I felt they had done with me.

"When she was thirteen, my parents emigrated to Europe and she did not want to go. She wanted to come and live with me instead. My parents would not allow it. Although she is in Europe, I feel very close to her. When my first daughter was born I kept making the mistake of calling her by my sister's name. Sometimes I think they are the same person." The arrow is a symbol of masculinity. In these words we understand the masculine principle coming forth, wanting to protect and guide the future life of the sister. After all, in many ways Kenneth brought her into life and feels fatherly towards her.

ABSTRACT

An abstract portion of a drawing or a whole abstract drawing usually represents either something that is hard to understand, difficult or abstruse, or an avoidance. The person may not know what he is concealing in the abstraction, but often, when asked, "What does this look like to you, or remind you of?" he will make important associations to some problem that he could not draw realistically. When a person draws many abstract pictures, perhaps he is running away from an issue, avoiding something, or it is unconscious content that needs to be worked on to be recognized.

Fig. 67

This impromptu drawing by Laura, age twenty-four, looks like a mandala. In Oriental art and religion, the mandala, usually symmetrical and circular, is a symbol of the universe.

Laura associated the designs in the aqua area to vaginas, and the ones in the blue area to sperm. She associated these sperm and the vagina with the use of sex for control. Then she told of being forced to have an abortion before her marriage. She is angry because her fiancé could not understand her need to bear the child. Also, she is angry with herself for being so much under his control that it was possible for him to persuade her to have the abortion.

Bill is eight years old and has leukemia, but his doctors say he does not know he has this serious illness and instructed me not to tell him. Bill draws this picture and tells me these are bubbles and "the bubbles can't reach the other bubbles" anymore. They get plugged up. A clogging occurs because of dirt and they cannot travel on as before. In his language he tells of cells which are not able to heal; he describes his ill-

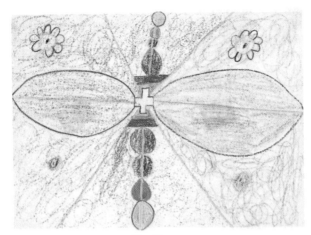

Fig. 68

ness and yet the medical personnel believe he doesn't know his diagnosis. I agree he doesn't know it on their terms, with their vocabulary, but he "knows" at some level. Here the abstract drawing, again following the individual's associations, gives insight into his psychology.

This drawing could also be viewed as a butterfly. A butterfly changes from a caterpillar, through the state of dissolution, to a winged creature. Its stages of development are life, death, and resurrection. Bill seems to "know," at some level, of his journey.

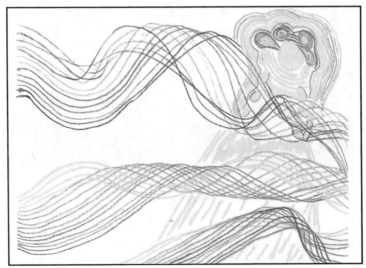

Fig. 69

This abstract impromptu drawing by Ethel, thirty-five, shows many colored lines interweaving. Ethel's first association to these abstract lines was sound waves. This led to discussion of her hearing loss and the trauma involved, its consequences and outcome. She is partially deaf and wears a hearing aid.

Her second association to this design was spiritual. Ethel finds to her surprise that she is moving into a more spiritual life and feels she is in communication with a higher power. She wonders if she is not "all in this world" at times, but finds this spiritual pull so strong she cannot deny it. Recently her Rabbi even asked her to interpret a psalm from the Old Testament and speak about it in the synagogue. She agreed and now finds she is growing more and more toward an even deeper experience with God.

FILLED IN VERSUS EMPTY

The drawing can be looked at as the individual's life, in a sense. Is it filled in or empty? How is the space used? Patients who are physically ill or psychologically lacking energy may not be able to fill the page. On the other hand, the page might be over-filled by a person whose energy is overflowing or who is perhaps overcompensating.

Fig. 70

In this spontaneous drawing, Frank, age six, fills all of the bottom part of the page with ground. Upon this he places trees, mountains, a very large cat and a rainbow with a sun in the upper right hand corner. The full page indicates vitality and interaction with life. Frank was a healthy child with lots of enthusiasm and was in the first grade at the time of this drawing.

In this impromptu drawing, Alan, age six, draws a stadium and tells me a story about how the stadium can be used for baseball and then changed to be used for football. I wonder where all the people are and why the rest of the page is blank. I equate this emptiness with the fact that Alan has leukemia and seldom has energy to complete tasks.

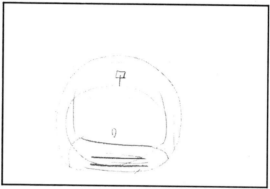

Fig. 71

In this impromptu drawing by Joan, forty-eight, we see the whole page used and colorfully filled in. Joan was enthusiastic about life, wanting

Fig. 72

to discover and learn all she could. She was at the beginning of a second career and was excited about its possibilities, and her energy level and enthusiasm were very high. We see the energy of the waves hitting the beach — a possible representation of Joan's inner energy.

Fig. 73

In the RKFD by Isabel, fifty-two, we see most of the picture on the right side of the paper, leaving a large space empty and void. Isabel is suffering from paralysis of her left side and her physical energy is limited, as reflected by the limited extent of her drawing.

TREES AND AGE

Looking at a tree as a life-symbol, one should ask if the tree is balanced, if it is healthy, or if its leaves can provide photosynthesis for the tree. We look for its rootedness and grounding in the earth.

The "life line" is drawn vertically from the base of the tree to the top of the crown, and notable markings on the tree — such as cut-off limbs, wounds, holes, height where foliage begins, broken branches, and so forth — should be noted and correlated to the age of the patient. Questions about these time periods corresponding to markings on the tree reveal significant information from the person's unconscious.

Placement of a bird's nest in the Apple Tree Drawing reveals significant data about Alice's life. Alice was asked to draw herself picking an apple from an apple tree, and she drew the tree with flowers at the bottom,

Fig. 74

herself picking an apple, and a bird's nest in the tree.

When viewing a tree as an *arbor vitae*, a tree of life, the therapist divides the tree from its base to its top according to the patient's age. In this case, Alice was twenty-six years old at the time of the drawing. Dividing the tree into twenty-six sections shows us the bird's nest is unconsciously positioned in Alice's nineteenth year of life. Alice says: "My parents were divorced, my mother had a nervous breakdown, and I cared for my younger sisters. In retrospect, there was turmoil in the home from my seventeenth to twentieth years. It does seem I took on the role of the mother bird." Evaluating further, we find that the space from the bottom of the bird's nest to the top of the mother bird's head correlates with Alice's seventeenth to twentieth years of life. These years were significant for Alice. Such turmoil and wounding, which hit her at a very deep level, need attention and care.

This amusing Apple Tree Drawing shows how a sixty-year-old man responded to "draw yourself picking an apple from an apple tree." He is a talented, energetic Puer type (forever young), who wears a business suit for almost all occasions and would not hesitate shinnying up a tree "dressed to the teeth" if that is what would be required to reach his goal.

When this creative man plans a new project, the priority goal becomes dominant in his life, consuming all his time and appearing bigger than life, just like the bigger than life apple. He is a multi-talented man and he could have just stood on the ground to catch the fruit of his labor.

Instead, in this drawing, he rushes to a perilous position to catch the giant-sized apple in the nick of time. It is also interesting to note that he may have felt desperate because that one apple was the only fruit on his tree. This desperate feeling will be a good area for his personal analytic work.

Fig. 75

The positioning of a tree knot, placed "decoratively" on the trunk of this apple tree, reveals significant information about Alexandra, fifty-three. We find the tree knot falls between ages seven and ten in Alexandra's life. In psychotherapy, Alexandra recalled a repetitious nightmare with Oedipal overtones during those years, with the stress culminating

Fig. 76

in facial tics during her tenth year. Tension had significantly subsided by the time Alexandra turned eleven. In that year, Alexandra had her first menstrual period and the first apple "grew" on her tree. Alexandra draws herself pointing to this first apple. Incidentally, we note that there are eleven apples on this tree. Alexandra reported, "Becoming a woman must have been highly significant for me."

DRAWING THE WORK SITUATION
WITHIN A FAMILY DRAWING

When a person is requested to draw a family picture and he includes his work situation, he is usually trapped by his work. Why is he so caught? Could it be that the family does not provide adequate relationships and that the work situation must compensate for this? Or is so much time spent away from the family that the individual begins to see work as an extension of family relationships? When work situations are included it

Fig. 77

is revealing to discover family relationships and emotional ties.

This RKFD recalls Andrea's days as a five-year-old. She places herself next to her mother, who is washing a pan at the kitchen sink. Her sister and brother are at the other end of the room, sitting and standing. Father is in the airplane above the open-ceilinged room. He was an air force pilot. As a child, Andrea felt that her father's profession and work were far more important to him than the family. Andrea said, "I do not remember bonding with him, or that he ever recognized me as a person with thoughts and feelings. As a result, I felt isolated and unprotected."

Fig. 78

In this KFD, Elaine draws herself at her desk working at her office. Her husband is cutting wood for the fireplace and her grown daughter is driving a car. Elaine is occupied with her world of work and she relates that sometimes this bothers her—that her work "eats the family time." Because of her work, Elaine does not live at home, but seventy miles away. Her life "revolves around work, study and personal social life." Elaine confided that her move seventy miles from her husband "began for school and work purposes, but the reality of the situation was incompatability with him."

FIVE-YEAR-OLD DRAWING TO PRESENT-DAY DRAWING

A drawing by an adult of how he remembers his family situation at age five often sheds light on how this person sees his past. He will frequently make present-day decisions based on past experiences. Comparing the content in a person's five-year-old drawing to a present-day drawing reveals how that person may be repeating childhood ways and not responding to a new environment and new individuals in the adult world.

In this RKFD by Ingrid, age forty-two, we see Ingrid feeding the chickens and her mother sewing in the backyard. Father is working in the garden and mother and fence block Ingrid from getting close to her father. Ingrid desired more communication with her father—she wanted to love him and wanted his love and closeness—but her relationship with her mother kept this from materializing.

Fig. 79

Fig. 80

In the KFD (figure 80), Ingrid, who is single, places herself four times
in the drawing. No central figures in the picture are masculine and we

can assume that a strong relationship with the masculine still does not exist in her life as a grown woman. This could easily be caused by the unrelatedness of the masculine principle earlier in her life. We see her (1) alone, (2) inside the large silhouette of mother, (3) with friends, and (4) washing windows. The pattern of the five-year-old is repeated. Ingrid needs to go back and learn how to relate to her father or to another masculine figure; then the masculine could develop in her life.

In this RKFD, we see Hilda, age forty-two, riding a horse with her sister. Hilda reports her father was "in reality a dreamer, philosopher, involved in studies of religion, mysticism, etc., was handsome and oozed sexuality." Mother was trapped in the housewife role. Hilda felt closer to her father and spent many hours with him in his library/laboratory discussing intellectual and spiritual pursuits. Now, as an adult, Hilda says that "only recently have I become aware of the psychological incestuous side of our relationship."

Fig. 81

In Hilda's KFD, we discover anxiety in the home. Hilda's youngest son just underwent open heart surgery. Her husband has changed professions from psychologist to contractor to professor to designer. Hilda describes him as "such a dreamer." Hilda feels trapped and confused about her role as mother versus professional. She says, "my oldest son is sensitive, a feeling type, and identified with me; my younger son identifies with his father." Hilda is now aware of psychological incestuous feelings toward her older

Fig. 82

son. The RKFD repeats itself thirty seven years later in this KFD. Even the words are the same in describing patterns of behavior. Hilda needs to understand that she married her father and is repeating the pattern of her parents' life. It is interesting to note the trajectory of the tractor and horse (father and daughter) in the RKFD, compared to the trajectory of the bicycle to the woman sitting under the tree (son and mother) in the KFD. The pattern is repeated years later.

LAYING PICTURES OVER EACH OTHER

When drawings are produced in a sequence, it is sometimes revealing to place them on top of each other, hold them to the light, and see what comes through. Putting these pictures together is often informative, offering new insights into a person's psychology.

In this RKFD, figure 83a, by Anna, age thirty-two, we see mother standing in the living room holding a wooden spoon with a hole in it and a frying pan that has no food in it. She is out of place and should be in the kitchen. I wonder how useful mother is: having a hole in her spoon, an empty frying pan in her hand, and standing with these implements in the living room. I question if mother is a very positive figure. However, Anna said, "For me the focus was on the negative aspects of dad." Then she added, "Drawing this picture gave me a headache."

Fig. 83a

Fig. 84a

In figure 83b, an impromptu drawing, Anna did a few abstract designs. The heart shaped, zig-zag lines in the lower right she associated with anger. The blue spiral and the yellow is associated with aspects of the feminine—"the yielding, the strength, the shell." The red triangle is seen as some aspect of "my feminine sexual self, or perhaps as an aspect of seizures or frequent headaches which begin at the base of my neck on my right."

Overlaying these two pictures we discover the red-blue-yellow zig-zag lines that Anna associates with anger are under mother. Anna was surprised and said, "I was originally going to draw mother with red shoes, but I censored that." She censored the color red because she felt red meant anger. One wonders how much anger she can censor toward her mother. She added, "It looks as if these lines will 'burn her legs.'"

The tall, dark black line going upward divides Anna in half. In reality Anna seems to be split on the issue of anger toward mother and father. The blue spiral and yellow line that she associated with the feminine aspect—"the yielding, the strength, the shell"—go through Anna and her siblings. Yielding, strength, and shell are what her siblings represent to her, and we see that she and her siblings are in alignment.

The purple cloud, as Anna describes it, is over her mother's head. Does her view of mother cloud her? Clouds have a tendency to represent anxiety in a drawing (Jacks, 1969), so I wonder if her mother produces anxiety in Anna's life. Anna then told me that the green eye is associated with the critical father issues. By overlaying these pictures, we find insights into family relations truly stemming from unconscious levels.

In this RKFD, figure 84a (page 94) by Bonnie, age twenty-eight, we see mother and brother in the house, father sideways and alone on the far left, and Bonnie alone on the steps. Her dog, under the tree, is her closest companion.

In the next picture, a KFD, Bonnie sits with her daughter reading a book. Again the dog is nearby. Here we have mother and daughter sharing, much unlike what Bonnie experienced in her childhood as shown in the first drawing.

Laying these drawings over each other, we find Bonnie as a five-year-old child overlapping the dog in the second drawing. The dog, symbolizing instincts, represents Bonnie's strong instinctual side. The figure of Bonnie today coincides with the figure of her own mother. Bonnie told me about this "indicating some concerns with mothering," either being like her mother or not being like her mother in her relationship with her own little girl.

---

*Note: If pages 94 and 96 are held to light overlaying aspect will become apparent.

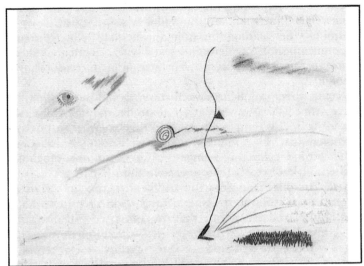

Fig. 83b

Fig. 84b

TRANSLATING COLOR

To write about the meanings of colors is an enormous undertaking. Many theories exist regarding the possible significance of colors, as do many books on color symbolism and the use of color, of which *The Luscher Color Test* by Max Luscher (1969) and *Color Personality: A Manual for the Color Pyramid Test* by Schaie and Hess (1964) are two prominent examples.

Different theories on color interpretation do not always agree on specific meanings, but theorists agree that colors can symbolize certain feelings, moods, even the tone of a relationship. The use of a particular color and its placement in a drawing may suggest a balance or imbalance in our lives. Colors may indicate the importance of psychological and/or physical factors. We cannot limit ourselves only to psychological factors with color interpretation. Somatic factors having an important effect on the individual's life will appear in the drawings, and these can manifest themselves in color or via another focal point.

Color analysis can be used as a supplementary aid in understanding drawings, though colors are often difficult to interpret accurately and may be misunderstood by the lay person. Although "a little knowledge can be a dangerous thing," applying interpretations for the colors we use need not be dangerous if we are objective. Color interpretation needs to consider how the color is used, where it is used on the page, quantity of the color used, what objects or material the color is used on, and the intensity of color displayed.

For example, the color red could mean energy, hate, a "burning" problem, danger, physical illness (fever, infection), love, joy, excitement and perhaps more. If I find red on a Valentine heart, it may mean love and care as opposed to finding the same quantity of red when displayed as drops of blood dripping from a threatening knife. This gives us a bit more insight as to why color interpretation has no cut and dried rules. It also demonstrates one reason for the diverse color theories that abound today. Another reason for the diversity of color interpretation is that color meanings vary from one culture and society to another. Many variables need to be considered in the use of color interpretation.

It is most helpful to come back to the world of nature when dealing with the significance of color — for example, green in healthy plant leaves and grass certainly tells us that the growing potential within the plant is good. The steadiness of a brilliant yellow sun, our greatest source of energy, light and warmth, may also reveal similar contents in a drawing.

Listed below are some common interpretations of color based upon the psychology and associations of Western culture. These findings are based mainly on Bach's work (1969, pp. 18-19). Furth (1973) and Williams (1985) have added to them. These color interpretations are especially interesting because they are compiled from the drawings of seriously ill patients.

Red — Psychologically, it may signal an issue of vital significance, a "burn-ing" problem, surging emotions, or danger. Physically, it may reflect an acute illness—for example, infection or fever.

Pink—As a lesser hue of red, it may suggest the resolution of a prob-lem or illness just past, where one now feels "in the pink." Often it is used for coloring flesh or cheeks to show the "healthy look" that we see portrayed in advertisements for cosmetics.

Purple — May point to a need to possess or control, or a need to have others control and support. It may suggest a burdensome responsibility, or indicate that one has a "cross to bear." Physically, it may indicate sei-zures or a controlling, gripping situation. As the royal or regal color, it suggests sovereignty, spirituality, supreme power (whether taken psycho-logically or somatically).

Orange — May reflect a suspenseful situation, especially a life-or-death struggle; it may also indicate decreasing energy or rescue from a threatening situation.

Golden Yellow— May suggest an emphasis on things of a spiritual or intuitive nature; something of great value. The yellowness of the sun may imply life-giving energy.

Pale Yellow—May indicate a precarious life situation.

Bright Blue — May denote health; the vital flow of life ("life's spring"), or energy.

Pale Blue — May denote distance, the far away, pale blue sky; a fading away or withdrawing; contemplation.

Dark Green—A healthy ego and body; growth or a newness of life, as in the healing process.

Pale Yellow-green — Psychological or physical weakness; a fading out of life or coming back into life, with the aid of treatment.

Dark Brown — Nourishment; in touch with nature and the terrestrial; healthy.

Pale Brown — May denote rot or decay, or a struggle to overcome destructive forces and return to a healthy state.

Black— May indicate or symbolize the unknown. If used for shading, it is generally seen as negative, projecting "dark" thoughts, a threat, or fear.

White —As the absence of color, may indicate repressed feelings; it may also, after all colors are used, signal life's completion.

Colors do not tell the story of a picture, they merely amplify what the objects and action within the picture have to say. To understand the rela-tive value or importance of colors in picture analysis, consider viewing a black and white television versus a colored one. In either case, the *basic* meaning of the program comes through.

While colors are not always of critical importance, Jolande Jacobi report-ed that Carl Jung "attaches as much importance to color and design as to what the images represent" (Jacobi 1980, p. 97).

With this as background, color used out of place, following color through a patients' picture series, colors missing within a drawing, and intensity of color are focal points worth noticing.

COLOR OUT OF PLACE

Color out of place is odd and needs to be noted and studied. A black sun, a green cow, or a purple person are all examples of colors out of place. What meaning does this displacement of color bring to the symbol?

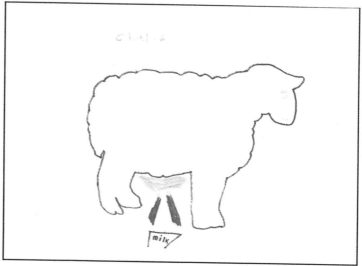

Fig. 85

A spontaneous drawing by Charles, age five, is actually a cut-out of a lamb from a drawing book. Charles added the red milk. He has leukemia and demonstrates his need for good, healthy, life-giving blood as his necessary "milk" of life. Red is a color of energy and vitality. It is interesting to note his appropriate use and placement of it.

Most notable in this impromptu drawing are the thirteen purple telephone poles. Jenny, age thirty-eight, is a Catholic. The color purple is spiritual and regal in nature. Thirteen crosses make me wonder about the fourteen stations of the cross. Where is the fourteenth cross which represents resurrection?

Jenny reported that she is beginning to be more aware of her spiritual belief system in the "deep recesses of [her] mind." She believes the purple crosses represent her need to communicate with her spiritual foun-

Fig. 86

dation, letting go of the suffering and allowing needed time for trans-figuration and resurrection.

Jenny bears several crosses. She has suffered problems with her mother and her mother's illness, problems of family life, and strife in her relationship with her husband. Jenny reported she has been married for twenty years and has just recently discovered her intense love for her husband. She is delighted with the insight, as is her husband.

Chapter 5

If we begin with certainties, we shall end in doubts;
but if we begin with doubts, and are patient in them,
we shall end in certainties.
— Bacon

Throughout my years of teaching and using drawing analysis, I have noticed a recurring problem that plagues students in their attempt to develop skill in this therapeutic technique. A student gets caught or trapped by the picture, becomes locked into one aspect of it, and cannot see the whole picture. The reason for this occurrence is that a vulnerable side of the student's personality gets hooked by some part of the picture so that some of the student's own unresolved psychic contents are set into play. These "vulnerable sides" are our own complexes, and we must always remain aware that these parts of ourselves are easily projected onto others without our conscious intent to do so. The student must be both conscious and wary of this danger so that the inner self does not get carried away and cause what truth there is in a drawing to be obscured.

Before a therapist can effectively help a patient with the symbolic language of his unconscious, the therapist must open the closet of his own unconscious and become acquainted with its contents. You are only one person, but within you there are many "persons." Within all of us there is a nurturing mother, a guardian father, a playful child, a happy person, a sad one, a wanderer, a settler. I could go on with a long list, but we can imagine all who live within us simply by acknowledging all the types of people around us. We are each a little bit of every one of them and

101

they are a bit of us as well. The "ones inside" are the "persons" from whom we must seek information, especially when we find ourselves hooked by something within a picture.

A short illustration may explain this. A professional therapist attended one of my workshops, wanting to learn how to use pictures in her work. She worked along with the group, but could not get beyond seeing only sexual problems in pictures. We discussed this privately and I wondered who inside her may have been caught in a sexual problem. I inquired into her puberty years and discovered she had experienced incestuous relations with her father and brother for four of these years. For several days she and I met, delving into this entanglement in her life, trying to sort through ideas and feelings of a pubescent girl's life. The pubescent girl was the "person" inside this professional who was caught in seeing only the sexual side of pictures. She took on the formerly hidden "person inside," who helped her to grow, and with time, she overcame her problem and began reading pictures for what they represented.

Looking for Road Signs

Throughout the therapeutic process, one should look for road signs to direct picture reading. Road signs must be considered along with road conditions. That is, if a road sign says to take a curve at forty miles per hour, and it is an inclement day in mid-winter and the roads are treacherous with ice, the driver needs to travel slower than the posted speed. The road signs guide, but the good therapist also takes into consideration the patient's current weather conditions. One may be guided by certain signs within a picture, but one must also consider the individual as a unique person.

To my surprise, I have observed that students who want to use pictures as a therapeutic tool sometimes forget that they are working with a human being, a living person—a being with feelings as well as a thinking mechanism of a brain. We need to remember that pictures are a tool for working with the patient as a whole person. In the process of using pictures, we translate for the patient what he has presented on paper. In so doing, it is easy to fall into cognitive interpretation, avoiding the feeling side of the individual. Figure 87 illustrates this point.

Fig. 87

It is obvious that the lawnmower could run over the woman in the picture. The man pushing the lawnmower drew the picture. The woman is his wife, weeding the lawn. While he and I discussed the general makeup of this picture, I attempted to sense his attitude toward his wife. I tried to become aware of his feelings about their relationship and to discover why he drew a lawnmower between them. Also, I tried to understand why he might feel a need to run her over. To do this I became alerted to what this pictorial expression might have held; however, I did not take my ideas and thrust them upon him. First, I see what ideas the pictorial expression might entail, then I try to remember that this picture could have a meaning other than what I think I see in it.

It is not necessary for therapists to share all their ideas. When people must share all they think they see, they may have an inner need to predict, to be a prophet for other lives. I have observed students, after reading a picture, bombarding the patient with questions like a matador might spear a bull. Where is the patient? Is he ready for all these questions? Let us return to the man with the lawnmower. What if his reason for seeking a therapist is because his wife died suddenly a few weeks prior to this initial session, and the therapist is not yet aware of this fact? It would not prove beneficial to ask immediately why he is trying to mow her down.

The Human Being, Not the Machine

The wise therapist remembers that the patient is there to become more aware of his problems and to discover for himself how to live and deal with these concerns as he sees fit. If we, as counselors, had only to inform patients of their problems and possible solutions to these problems, we could write a reference book entitled "Counselors' Recipes for Living." This would be an easy remedy, but unfortunately it is not realistic. In therapy situations with human beings, "recipes" simply do not work. In C.G. Jung's words,

> It is enough to drive one to despair that in practical psychology there are no universally valid recipes and rules. There are only individual cases with the most heterogeneous needs and demands — so heterogeneous that we can virtually never know in advance what course a given case will take, for which reason it is better for the doctor to abandon all preconceived opinions. This does not mean that he should throw them overboard, but that in any given case he should use them merely as hypotheses for a possible explanation. (Jung 1966, *CW* 16, p. 71).

Through this search for problems and solutions, quite a bit of information must be learned by the patient. Someday, one hopes, the patient will be capable of going off on his own to encounter future problems and dilemmas with a better ability to study them and resolve them successfully by using skills and observations introduced by the therapist. With the skills learned and used in the sessions, he will have discovered a process for finding his way through future problems. Therefore, it is important to be alert to the fact that solving problems in the present is only half the remedy, and the second half at that. The first half is helping another person discover a method, his method, to respond to and deal with problems — present problems and problems of the future.

The Patient's Path

In analyzing pictures, the therapist reads what the picture may be saying and takes these insights as clues toward phrasing questions for the patient to consider; then we must travel the road the patient travels. The therapist can "store" his thoughts and questions, since time may come in another session when these can be brought to light. There have been many times in working with a patient that I have had ideas, questions, possible insights to problems, but the patient traveled elsewhere, and I found in the next session (or several sessions later) that the patient came back to the issue and I could say: "I recall this from the picture you drew last month. Could you tell me more about this?" or "How does this fit into your life now? or "How did it fit into your life then?"

> One has to remind oneself again and again that it is more important in ther-
> apy for the patient to understand than for the analyst's theoretical expecta-
> tions to be satisfied. The patient's resistance to the analyst's interpretation
> is not necessarily wrong; it is rather a sure sign that something does not 'click.'
> Either the patient has not yet reached the point where he understands, or
> the interpretation does not fit. (Jung 1964, p. 61).

In allowing a patient to travel his "path," the most common road sign
the therapist may encounter is the stop sign. The therapist must be aware
that when he interrupts the patient, he is essentially stopping the patient from "traveling." This does need to be done occasionally, but I have
observed students interrupting patients because the students are not getting answers to their questions. Perhaps an answer is in the avoidance
of answering. The avoidance serves a purpose and should not be ignored.

Befriending Our Defense Mechanisms

A great error therapists frequently make is wanting patients to rid themselves of all defense mechanisms. I advocate holding onto these defensive
mechanisms and admiring them. I view defense mechanisms as very pre-
cious materials. They may vary in size, but I help the patient examine
his defense mechanisms not to rid himself of them, but instead to admire them, touch them, polish them, become better acquainted with
them, to befriend them. As therapy progresses, movement beyond this
defense mechanism takes the person to the next one, while old defense
mechanisms get placed in a "tabernacle," always ready to be brought out
for use if necessary, and always available for a "visit" when needed. Eventually, the patient experiences no need to "visit" or to "polish" an old
defense mechanism. He thus gets a better understanding of how to face
his defense mechanisms, and this understanding becomes his best teacher and friend in confrontations with other unconscious materials.

A participant in one workshop was a newly ordained minister assigned
to temporary duty in a rural community. Within days of his arrival in
the community, one of its oldest members died. He was called to her
death bed immediately, though he did not know the woman. He went
to call, wishing most vehemently that the old woman had not died at
that precise time. Upon arriving at the deceased's home, he said a few
prayers with all the old-timers present. After this ritual he was left in
a silent void. What was he to say? Not knowing anyone, how could he
give reassurance to these people? How was he to communicate with them?
He thought that if only he knew them it would be easier to console them.
He was bewildered and wished to be out of there; instead, he found this
community waiting for his words of wisdom.

I asked this newly ordained minister what he had most wanted to do in this situation. He responded that he wanted to run away. Why did he want to run? Most likely because he felt he could not find any answers for the mourners. But is it answers they really wanted? The therapist should try to determine what questions the runner has, what the runner needs to know. If the runner only knew what this woman had done for the community, he could have praised her for having helped many people. If the runner only knew about the good she had done, he could have spoken about her more honestly. If the runner only knew how this woman had loved, how she became the "center of the community," how this world had become a better place because of her—if the runner only knew. I suggested that the minister "take on the runner." Here is where the so-called enemy becomes a friend.

I would have preferred the minister to speak the truth about his feelings: "I am young and so new to this community, I don't know what to say. I want to console you, but I did not know this woman. If you would only tell me the things she did for this town, how she helped you in your lives, what she added to the growth of this community, how long she had been here—I know nothing of her except that she must have been quite some person." Responses would have been forthcoming and, because those around would then be able to share their loss, a healing process would have begun. Thus, the runner inside might have taken on his task, and in so doing, have become a friend to the young minister.

Probing versus Pushing

There have been occasions when I observed a therapist pressuring a patient into answering questions that were suggested by the picture. It may be a good idea to tape therapeutic sessions occasionally and listen to what one is doing. If the session invariably becomes a question/answer period, one should step back and analyze what is happening. A basic premise is that to work with pictures in therapy, one must be aware of one's own individuality. Otherwise the patient's problems will never be dealt with, only the therapist's, and this is not why the patient came to therapy. Jung refers to this when he writes that:

> Medicine in the hand of a fool was ever poison and death. Just as we demand from a surgeon, besides his technical knowledge, a skilled hand, courage, presence of mind, and power of decision, so must we expect from an analyst a very serious and thorough psychoanalytic training of his own personality before we are willing to entrust a patient to him. I would even go so far as to say that the acquisition and practice of the psychoanalytic techniques presuppose not only a specific psychological gift but in the very first place a serious concern with the moulding of one's own character. (Jung 1961, CW 4, p. 450).

Jung continues:

An analyst can help his patient just as far as he himself has gone and not a step further. In my practice I have had from the beginning to deal with patients who got 'stuck' with their previous analysis, and this always happened at the point where the analyst could make no further progress within himself. (Jung 1966, *CW* 16, p. 545).

From what I have ascertained, this is the main reason that projective tests have not yet developed as productive counseling tools. They are very informative, but the therapist must be alert not to project his problems onto the patient's drawing. This safeguard cannot be achieved without first knowing oneself, but given the pace of contemporary society, it seems therapists and students of psychology never take time to find out about their own lives first. Instead, they go immediately into the therapy of others before they have experienced introspection and therapy for themselves. This is unfortunate for both the development of the therapist and for the patients.

Professional Jargon

While working in a large hospital, I met a personable physician who worked very closely with his patients. Hospitalized at this time was Mrs. Lincoln, an elderly lady from a lower-middle class background. We had many good times together and she informed me early that she had carcinoma, diagnosed and originally cared for by this personable physician. Mrs. Lincoln had many unkind words about the doctor, which surprised me. For nine months she was unaware of the seriousness of her illness; she knew only that she had a carcinoma but did not know this meant cancer. One day she decided to go to the library and gather additional information about her disease. Upon discovering what her illness was, she felt betrayed by the doctor for not telling her all the "facts." Thereafter, she was unable to work successfully with him. The doctor, on the other hand, felt he had been honest, open, and supportive throughout her illness and had difficulty grasping her misunderstanding.

It seems to me that language that is understood is more important than professional jargon. I would even further suggest that occasionally it may behoove the therapist to ask the patient to explain his situation, giving an insight into the patient's understanding of the circumstances. Perhaps if Mrs. Lincoln had been asked to explain her understanding of her illness to her physician, he would have caught on that she did not understand carcinoma. For the physician, this misunderstanding shielded him during the many months Mrs. Lincoln was unaware of the seriousness of her illness, but it eventually led to a hindrance in the physical care he could give her.

In the literature of analytical psychology, we find such words as shadow, anima, animus, archetype, typology. To Jung the discovery of the content of these words, their meaning, their significance was not an easy task. It took time and hard work. And this was not accomplished intellectually alone, but painfully felt. Therapists do little good to use professional jargon or vocabulary with patients. To learn the meaning of these words, the patient needs to "feel" the discovery of these words, their significanse and how their meaning fits into life. The use of the vocabulary blocks this inner discovery. The therapist denies the patient the privilege of struggling toward self-discovery if his psychology is put into universal jargon. It becomes an intellectual experience and misses the "soul." As Barbara Hannah reports, to be a successful therapist we must learn to "think in our heart—not in our mind" (Hannah 1976, p. 159).

Negatives are Negative and Positives are Positive

To do valid work with pictures, one must believe that negative aspects of a neurosis are negative. It seems we are, at present, facing a sort of contradiction. We seem willing to see the dark side of a circumstance, but only for its positive value. Then we confuse ourselves by uttering platitudes such as "all negatives are positive." This statement naturally seems to ring true because we are allowing ourselves to look only at the positive side of the darkness. This is a romantic attitude.

Nature ordains that positives and negatives have a right to co-exist. For example, a family may be brought closer together when the father suffers an accident that renders him quadraplegic. The cooperation and support generated among family members is a positive outcome; the impact of the quadraplegia upon the man's marriage and his career, however, is a negative aspect that cannot be ignored.

What about the other half, which may hold reality for the negative side of the darkness? Frequently it is shrugged off before it is properly analyzed. Could it be we are not capable of handling negative aspects? Jung reminds us to look at both sides and writes on this in reference to a neurosis:

> A neurosis is by no means merely a negative thing, it is also something positive. Only a soulless rationalism reinforced by a narrow materialistic outlook could possibly have overlooked this fact. In reality the neurosis contains the patient's psyche, or at least an essential part of it; and if, as the rationalist pretends, the neurosis could be plucked from him like a bad tooth, he would have gained nothing but would have lost as much as the thinker deprived of his doubt, or the moralist deprived of his temptation, or the brave man deprived of his fear. To lose a neurosis is to find oneself without an object; life loses its point and hence its meaning. This would not be a cure, it would be a regular amputation. (Jung 1970, *CW* 10, p. 167).

We devalue negative elements in an individual's life by trying to see only the positive. Is it the fear of finding the negative side of oneself that prompts us to do this? Why should we not find the bad side in ourselves and let it be bad? This foolish attempt to alter or change the negative in oneself is a denial of life. If we search only for the good, we live only part of life. One cannot change something unless it is accepted for what it is, as it is.

An example of this is the story of an obese woman I worked with. The negative elements in her needed to be respected, as they were making it impossible for anyone to love her, and eventually her husband and son left her. We found she had to take on this negative aspect, not try to make it positive, but to face what caused her to become the way she was before she could lose weight and begin to love again.

Negative traits need to be respected since they comprise a part of the psychic whole. There were probably very sound reasons for those traits to develop in the first place, and they should not be arbitrarily abandoned. Perhaps if we think this way we will not have to rid ourselves so quickly of negative traits because of dislike and fear. Negative aspects oftentimes are well earned through hard knocks, though it should not be forgotten that they may need to be changed after one has learned from them.

Let us consider anger as an element with both positive and negative aspects. To see it as having only positive or only negative attributes is to devalue it. I heard a student recently tell me anger was not good. I was a bit surprised, and asked the reason why. She could not say, except that she had been told by a previous instructor that anger was not serving a purpose, that it was only negativity and that she should rid herself of it. Interestingly, she added without a pause that she had observed the previous instructor becoming angry and she wanted to know how I could explain this.

It was indeed a question I could not answer, as I did not see anger as only negative or only positive. Anger serves a purpose. One considers anger as negative and does not allow it to surface; if one makes no attempting at discovering "who" inside oneself is angry, chances are that one will never grow into a total person. We can become aware of our anger, find out what it may mean, and learn to use it constructively. To deny it a right to exist or to fend it off as wasteful is detrimental to our growth as individuals. Anger, as a negative element, can teach us positive things.

Right-Handed Versus Left-Handed Drawings

One question often asked is whether a person's dominant handedness has any significance in drawing. Thus far, no significant differences between right-handed and left-handed individuals' portrayals or positionings in drawings have been found. The concept of the collective unconscious could account for this. The basic elements of nature, which are at the core of each person's psyche, may well be the same, regardless of handedness. Unconscious content can be extremely personal; however, archetypal content found in drawings tells us that there is a thread which originates in the collective unconscious. For example, in humankind's collective experience, the sun will rise in the east and set in the west, gravity will pull everything down, trees and plants tend to grow upward, and shape, color, size and direction of things will be the same for right- or left-handed individuals.

Quadrant Assessment Theories

Quadrant assessment simply means the division of a drawing into four equal parts, beginning with an axis in the center of the picture. Some theorists attribute specific meanings to these quadrants. I am apprehensive about this approach and not yet convinced of its validity and reliability. I want to talk briefly about quadrant theories here because I find many students attempting to use them as law.

In her work on tree drawings, Karen Bolander (1977, p.76) divides the page not into four equal parts, but into many components. Her findings certainly have impressed me because she works scientifically with a consistent variable — always the tree. With this consistency, she can research the use of the page more easily than with a spontaneous or impromptu drawing, which uses any amount of symbols on a page.

Susan Bach (1969, p. 16) has established findings on quadrant usage and her quadrant theory could be very helpful if applied to the same population from which it was derived. Her subject population was seriously ill children, and consequently it does not constitute a random sampling. To my knowledge this theory has not yet been tested with other populations.

Elisabeth Kübler-Ross has also developed a quadrant theory. It has not been tested on a random population either, but was devised from drawings of participants at her Life-Death-Transition Workshops and from her personal work with dying patients and bereaved families. Quadrant theory is included in the curriculum at The C. G. Jung Institute in Zürich, though I have not seen nor have I heard of any scientific studies to validate this particular approach.

When I see therapists reading and evaluating pictures by dividing them into quadrants and categorizing compartmentally rather than viewing the picture as a unified whole, I get concerned. It is important to keep in mind that images and their placement may not always reflect the same meaning. It is so easy to make a "recipe" of quadrant theory. For some reason many students of picture interpretation "grab hold" of quadrant theories and want to apply them. This is done far more frequently with quadrant study than with other focal points, such as color symbolism, movement within the drawing, perspective, use of space, counting repeated objects, and so forth. At this time I do not totally comprehend why this happens, yet I have observed this phenomenon occurring repeatedly in picture interpretation seminars. My hunch is that quadrant explanations are presented in an image form, whereas all the remaining focal points and/or guidelines are presented only in word form with examples. Images tend to "travel deeper" than words into the unconscious and perhaps this is a possible explanation.

A young colleague who graduated from a well-known institute of analytical psychology told me that he frequently analyzes pictures for psychological content. He said that one of the most important rules to remember is that the lower half of the picture is always the unconscious, while the upper half of the picture is always the conscious. He feels he can also designate a father complex or a mother complex by where particular figures are placed on the drawing page. Research data do not document this colleague's statement. I believe the only generalization I can make in dealing with the language of drawings is that no generalization can be made.

C. G. Jung wrote of having had a dream about going downstairs into the basement, later explaining this as a figurative journey into the unconscious (Jung 1963). For Jung and his dreams this interpretation could be true; it could even occasionally hold true for some drawings. However, it is not necessarily true for everyone all the time. Creating pictures, as well as weaving dreams, is a very personal experience. I prefer to list road signs rather than recommend a set of rules. I believe that being flexible and attuned to the uniqueness of each patient and the path each travels is more important.

This warning in mind, I will introduce the paper-division theory devised by I. Jolles (1977), which from my experience is both valid and reliable. One of the reasons I value this theory is because its results can be explained and understood, unlike the arbitrary conception of the young colleague mentioned above. In Jolles' theory, the drawing page is not divided into quadrants, but into halves. If within a drawing most of the content is drawn on the lower half of the page, Jolles considers the individual being reality-bound or concrete (Figure 88). An individual who is reality-bound sees hunger as a world problem, feels the threat of annihilation from a nuclear war always hanging overhead, and understands the economic instability in which we live. This reality-bound person will lean towards depression and will feel insecure and even inadequate in attempting to deal with the enormity of these reality issues. In contrast, the individual who draws most of his picture on the upper half of the drawing, according to Jolles, is more apt to be aloof and inaccessible. He tends to seek satisfaction in fantasy and needs grounding. He most likely strives toward but never quite reaches his always-unattainable goal.

```
Strives strongly although the
    goal is unattainable.
Seeks satisfaction in fantasy.
Keeps aloof, relatively inaccessable.

Feels insecure and inadequate.
Leans to depression.
Reality bound (concrete)
```

Fig. 88

```
Emotional                      Seeks satisfaction
    dominance.                     in intellectual
Impulsive.                         areas.
Stresses past.                 Controlled behavior.
                               Stresses future.
(Unconscious.)                 (Conscious)
```

Fig. 89

As in figure 89, a drawing placed toward the right half of the page as opposed to the left, or on the whole of the paper, leans towards consciousness. A conscious-bound individual is more able to control his behavior, can seek satisfaction in intellectual areas, and has a tendency to stress future events. Use of the left side of the paper tends to deal with unconscious content. A person who is unconscious is impulsive, and emotions can dominate his life. He tends to continuously deal with the past.

There are others theories of paper division, though I do not cite them because in my opinion their biases outweigh their significance. I urge caution regardless of the paper division theory one may decide to follow, and I urge the therapist to keep an open eye to the personal significance of each individual's placement of drawings on paper.

Chapter 6

*Read me what you write
or show me what you draw
and I'll tell you what you are.*
— *Emanuel F. Hammer*

The cases presented in this chapter will use Draw-A-Person, Draw-A-Man, and the impromptu drawing techniques. As defined earlier, an impromptu drawing is one which the patient draws immediately upon request and in which he has the freedom to draw whatever he desires. Later, I interpret the drawings as a pictorial language that tells me how to help the patient celebrate life.

These drawings and case studies are selected to give the reader a broader scope on the use of drawings. I concentrate only on the most significant aspects of each picture in order to illustrate what seems important to the client. This approach helps me to understand the patient's primary problem. This does not mean that other aspects of the drawings are not noteworthy; if I were to go into detail concerning all aspects of the drawings presented, I would probably need a chapter for each picture. I do, however, go into greater detail when I am working with a patient and his or her family.

Listening to the Picture

Since a picture has no vocal cords, I lend it mine and begin expressing aloud the story the picture reveals. I do not try to make sense out of it

113

at first. Figure 90 illustrates how this process works.

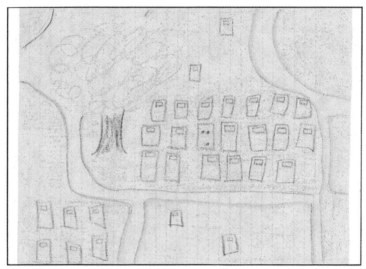

Fig. 90

The original picture, which has unfortunately been destroyed by the artist, was first given to me by a thirty-year-old Jewish woman at a workshop on death and dying. Upon viewing the picture, I asked myself if the tree in the upper left quadrant could be the patient's tree of life. In a cemetery that has many graves, there is one grave with three circles; it is almost in the center of the picture and it has no gravestone. It must be an important one to be placed so centrally and to have three circles, a feature shared by no other grave. There is also an empty plot nearby, whereas there are not many empty plots near the other graves. I wonder who is buried in this central, unmarked grave. I wonder why this one has no stone. The roads are twisting and winding; they are very narrow and the terrain is flat.

With this information, I may have some insight into what is happening to the woman who drew the picture. I am curious to know what would make her draw a cemetery; and especially, why that central, unmarked grave has three circles. What importance and significance does this have for her, and for whom is she possibly grieving? Whom is she burying, or whom is she not burying? Does the lack of a gravestone mean the denial of death, or simply not enough time to draw a stone on the grave? What is to be done with the nearby empty plots? These are questions and ideas that the picture elicited from me. We know that all art work is a means of communication, and we are pursuing the discovery of this communication from both the conscious and the unconscious within the individual. The task now is to put this picture into story form and try to make sense of what the picture says.

I then begin by assessing what is known. I know the picture is from a woman. She is Jewish. She is about thirty years of age. The majority of the picture is of a cemetery, so it most likely has something to do with death—hers or that of a loved one. The tombstone is an outer recognition of death, and most graves have tombstones. I can see that the woman who drew this picture has the ability to put tombstones on the graves. The fact that the central grave is missing its tombstone must be important. There is one dead person who does not have this recognition. Since the woman is Jewish, it could be that this is a recent death and that the gravestone will be placed, according to tradition, after the first anniversary of death. Are there other reasons for the missing gravestone? At this point I don't know.

There are definite markings on this centrally placed grave. They are not characteristic of any of the other graves; they are very special. But what do they represent to the woman who drew them? In counseling this individual, I would begin with whatever in her picture caught my attention, and thus help her unravel the trauma she must be experiencing within and expressing symbolically.

After I shared some of my general observations with her, the young woman offered the following information:

> This is a drawing of the cemetery where my father is buried. He abandoned our family when I was five, and I was to see him only once again, when I was six. My mother was very bitter about my father's desertion and never had a good word to say about him.
>
> "Yet he remained my 'knight in shining armor.' I remember making mud-pie cookies for him, going to the drugstore for a soda with him. . .little memories that I cherished, idolized. I always prayed he would return to us so that the family would be together again and mama would be happy.
>
> "This was not to be, however. As time passed, my mother found an ally in my brother, who also spoke of my father only in anger. I was the only one who seemed to love and miss him. Why had he left us? What was he really like? My father held all the answers, and he was gone.
>
> "When I reached adulthood I decided to search for him, secretly hoping he was searching for me, too. My fiancé encouraged my efforts, sensing this would be important to our relationship as well. My search eventually took us not into my father's arms to hear my questions answered, but instead to an unmarked grave in Florida. As is the Jewish custom, we placed two stones on the graves as our farewell."

Two of the circles were now explained. But what about the third circle? I wanted to ask about it, but I realized this was due to my curiosity, not because the young woman indicated that she was ready to relate her experience of visiting the grave of her father. I withheld the question, thinking that it would come up later. Here I want to point out again that it is very important not to be caught by the picture and one's own questions. The therapist must constantly remember that he is in contact with a human being and that the picture is only a vehicle for communicating with this person.

The young woman continued.

> "The other circle represents a cookie I had taken to place upon my father's grave. To me, it symbolized the mudpie cookies I baked for him as a child, a gift which always won his smiles. When I placed the cookie upon the grave, tears which must been wanting release for years poured forth. I began speaking to him in Yiddish, grieving not only for the seeming finality of my loss, but for all the lost years as well."

I am sure some excellent sharing went on between this woman and the aspect of her father still alive in her. What a wonderful opportunity for her! It reminds me explicitly that death cannot end a relationship between two people. As long as one person in the relationship is living, the relationship goes on, albeit in a different form.

The Stuttering Adult

Figure 91 shows how an adult stutterer illustrated his feelings through an impromptu drawing.

This was drawn by Sebastian, a twenty-five-year-old male who was an accomplished musician. He was naturally self-conscious about his stuttering. Sebastian was asked to draw pictures of himself, representing his feelings immediately before, during, and after a stuttering episode. At first he was apprehensive, not knowing what to draw and not knowing "how" to draw. He solved this by illustrating the flowing sequence of his feelings in one picture.

The movement in the picture is from the left to the right and is represented by a triangle. This flowing movement is very positive. Sebastian attempts to keep the theme of his feelings in a flowing movement within one drawing as compared to separate themes of his feelings in separate drawings. If it were in separate drawings, it could appear to be moving like a stuttering effect and this, of course, is something that Sebastian would like to work away from.

The triangle which Sebastian used as an abstract representation of Self has its apex pointed upward, and this usually indicates masculinity. The

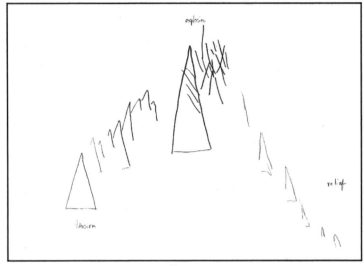

Fig. 91

triangle bounded by three straight lines leads us to think of any triad: father, mother, child; heaven, earth, human being; birth, life, death; the human being as body, soul and spirit. Thus, it is a unity of parts—multiplicity. Three is a number always moving towards four, which in numerical symbolism represents wholeness and totality. Three is creative power, as embodied by the three persons in the trinity. There are three gifts of the Magi to Christ; three temptations of Christ; three denials of Peter; three crosses on Calvary; three days of the death of Christ; three appearances of Christ after his death; and three theological virtues of Christianity—Faith, Hope and Love. This number three has many Christian references. Sebastian's father is a minister, a representative of The Great Father. As representative he must project an honorable, good, and superior image to the community. It is no wonder Sebastian felt conflict between himself and his earthly father as well as with The Great Father.

Let us look closely at these triangles and their labels. The first stage has a firmly drawn triangle that is almost complete. A small opening on the right side of the apex is visible. This drawing is representative of Sebastian's feeling before a stuttering episode comes on, and is labeled "tension." Sebastian said that he battled between the words "fear" and "tension" when trying to label this stage. So the anxiety and pressure begin to build. We then see the triangle is fragmented into eight segments as it advances and elevates to the second state of the stuttering experience.

The second triangle rises in height and is centrally positioned on the page. Here we have a real shattering or "explosion," as it is labeled. The pencil markings are darker, especially to the right of the central triangle, and we can feel from the reverse of the drawing paper that they were drawn with more pressure. Sebastian said that he has "odd feelings and aggression towards [himself]" which could be seen as exactly what the stuttering experience is doing to him. In the course of the analysis, he himself mentioned very nonchalantly that he is named after a famous martyr. Here again, Sebastian does have an impossible masculine role to emulate. He has a martyr for a namesake and model, which could encumber any human, both psychologically and somatically. It is very likely that this burden could be expressed somatically in his stuttering.

The third triangle is really a diminishing triangular design. It never regains its shape as it descends to the lower right hand corner of the drawing page. Even with six attempts to structure it, it cannot come together again. Finally, it rests at its lower place on the paper, broken, with no bottom, incomplete in form. The pressure is noticably lighter and limp. It is titled "relief" and Sebastian battled between the words " humble" and "relief." These words are the only ones available for the individual in such a situation. A person can only humble himself before God and his representative, the minister, which in this case was Sebastian's father. He can feel relieved in whatever he can accomplish, which of course would never be satisfactory for such a higher power. Relief could be felt because at least something was done in attempting to satisfy God and His representative. In the outer world, Sebastian took on the task of becoming a well-trained church musician. This was his way of working for God. He could not become a minister, like his father, because he claimed to have too many doubts and questions. Instead of confronting these questions and doubts, Sebastian avoided them, though his music at least partially compensated for his quest to work for the Church and God. (Toward the completion of his analysis Sebastian noted that his stuttering was subsiding; he had successfully begun resolving many of his unanswered questions).

Mirrors of a Psyche/Soma in a Leukemic Child

Now we will focus our attention upon a series of drawings I collected from a little girl who had leukemia. When I first saw six-year-old Teresa, she walked into the hospital with her mother. The family had traveled

Fig. 92

Fig. 93

Fig. 94

quite far to come here for Teresa's treatment. I remember how impressed I was with the mother's warmth and cheerfulness. I observed that Teresa was shy and small for her age. Her face was puffed beyond its normal size owing to fluid accumulation caused by her chemotherapy. She did not talk much, but her smile amply compensated for her reticence. It was easy to read her feelings just by following her expressions. When Teresa did talk, it was about her two sisters and three brothers and the fun they had together watching their favorite TV programs. Her chief joy was her family and the love they gave to her. Teresa would consider it a great sadness to have no one to play with; but with such a large and loving family this calamity was not likely to occur.

Figure 92 is the first of a series of three drawings by Teresa, which appear to be self-portraits. Almost all the leukemic children in my study drew figures that seemed to relate strongly to themselves.

In figure 92, we see a smiling girl standing on some kind of a base. I had observed how special Teresa seemed to her entire family, so I knew that in actuality there was firm support for this child. Notice that the legs, arms, body, and head are in fairly normal proportion to one another, and that the face is very round. But what especially absorbs my interest is the way that the tips of her toes and the top of her head form a connecting link between the ground and the sky. How can such a little one be touching both heaven and earth? Could we take this to indicate that her time is near? The next picture may give us more insight.

When Teresa arrived a month later at the clinic, she drew the picture we see in Figure 93. We learned that she was experiencing pain in her legs at this time. She commented that her drawing was her backyard and that the girl had been picking flowers. There were twelve flowers shown. I notice that the picture is symmetrical, with a tree on both sides, five flowers suspended on each side, and each hand holding one flower. Why should there be total of twelve flowers? Repeated objects often relate to a significant period of time in one's life. What I find frightening, however, is the position of the blue sky: In the first drawing it touches Teresa's head, but in figure 93 it becomes her grounding. To have "heaven above" is grand—all is in its place. But "heaven below" makes me concerned for the future. Is this movement of color just a childish whim? I don't think so.

Notice how the figure's legs are spindlier than in the former drawing, and that the face is out of proportion to the body. However, the smile on the face is still Teresa's smile.

After two months, Teresa returned to the clinic, this time on crutches. Her legs were giving her severe pain and she had difficulty moving them. She drew another picture for me (Figure 94).

The outdoor scene is gone now, and the figure's moon-shaped face occupies much of the page. Once again we see a reflection of the results of her chemotherapy. Not only had the drugs caused puffy edema to alter her appearance, but they had made her hair fall out as well. The arms and legs are very small extensions on this figure's body. In reality, Teresa's own limbs were small and useless. In fact, one week later, Teresa was carried into the hospital by her mother, and within a few weeks the child died.

It is interesting to note that whether by accident or coincidence—whichever one chooses to call it—twelve weeks after Teresa made her drawing containing the twelve flowers, she died.

Let us look again at Teresa's three extemporaneous drawings and compare them. Teresa's treatment of the figure's arms and legs show her actual prognosis of immobility before she became immobile. Following the series, we see that her body recedes in size, until her face is almost top-heavy, with the body too small to support her head. There is an interesting detail that appears in the last picture. Instead of one dot for a nose, the figure has two, representing nostrils. Teresa seems to be communicating to us her own awareness that her body is less supportive, and that she is focussing more on breath itself to stay alive. The smile remains on the figure. I have no reason to believe that Teresa's smile as she faced death was any less real than when she was healthier, secure all the while in her family's love. We can see that her drawings were mirrors of her psyche and soma. (The author thanks Elisabeth Kübler-Ross and Macmillan Press for permission to use this material).

It seems to me that both somatic and psychological information has been revealed through these impromptu drawings, stemming from the conscious and unconscious realms of the psyche. Information is frequently revealed through drawings, which either the professional may overlook in his regular sessions with the patient, or of which the patient himself is not consciously aware. These concerns are not necessarily overlooked on purpose. It is hard to know what is occurring in a patient's mind and to discover what are his greatest concerns.

A therapist cannot be expected to detect and understand every aspect of a patient's drawing in relation to psychological and somatic processes. But if there is a significant feature that has been expressed pictorially and yet goes unrecognized for what it actually represents, as with dreams, subsequent drawings will present the feature again and again, in various forms, until it becomes known at least to the therapist, if not to the patient himself. Hence, if the therapist heeds the premises and follows the suggestions I have made in this book, his patients will be helped by having their pictorial expressions transformed into useful tools for healing and promoting growth.

After reading the text, especially Chapter Four (Focal Points), it is easier to understand how most of the findings in the picture I mentioned in my introduction (Figure 95) were ascertained. There may be a few factors that are not yet clear.

I did not like my initial feelings when I first observed this drawing. They ranged from fright and shock to illness and devastation. I felt contained, closed off and too weak to do anything about what was happening to me. In short, I did not like the drawing and felt strongly that it was drawn by a physically sick patient who was encountering psychological difficulty. We now know both of these facts were true.

In the drawing, the body cavity is not closed off. It is bottle-shaped with an open bottom. On the right side of the body cavity we see large dark brown-black strokes. This is unusual, in terms of both color and color intensity, when compared with the other side of the cavity. I wondered what was happening in this part of the body cavity. Also, I noticed dark brown-black strokes similar to a stroke of coloring on the head. None are large strokes, but they are all definitely there. I supposed the physical illness to be where the odd brown-black coloring presented itself in the cavity, and perhaps it had metastasized to the head region. You will recall from the introduction that when I suggested this to the mother, she confirmed that her child had retroperitoneal sarcoma, a cancer inside the lining of the abdomen. However, she stated that the illness had not metastasized to the head. Near the end of our interview I escorted this

Fig. 95

woman, whom I admired for her inner courage in facing up to her abilities and inadequacies in such a trying time, out to her waiting husband. As we walked she told me of guilt feelings concerning her son's illness. She told me of his incredibly severe headaches and that nothing satisfactory could be done to alleviate them until a few weeks before his death. A fellow nurse had suggested an ice pack be used. This helped tremendously, but she regretted the time she wasted until this discovery. This gave me an answer to the color of the body cavity illness being repeated in the head region.

When I began work on the drawing, I was concerned with the child's age and sex. I thought developmental information would be helpful in understanding the child's life. From viewing a few thousand pictures over the past years, I assumed this drawing was by a child and not an adult. The body integration in this drawing give signals to me that the child would be almost five. However, whether the child was a boy or a girl was very difficult to discern. At first I thought it was a girl. The body is a bottle form, and symbolically the bottle is feminine. But this did not fit with another piece of information in the picture; the presence of very lightly drawn wing-like encapsulations around each hand. They are purple and basically enclose the arms and hands. Near the fingers, however, there is definitely a small opening on both sides. Purple, which could be seen as a color of possession, or in this case enclosure, seemed a strong indication to me that this child was being confined, held back, enclosed. The opening is not big enough for the hand to pass through. Purple also appears in the eyes and in the body container and if one looks very closely, the color delineates two breast nipples. They are very tiny, but definitely there. I wondered who or what was possessive, be it psychological or somatic. The color purple gives definition to a body part, the breast. This made me consider the feminine, and a child's major relationship with the feminine is through his mother. This brought to mind the Oedipal complex. I then considered the drawing to be from a little boy's world. If this is so, the mouth being drawn in this color and fashion (big and tightly closed) indicates he certainly did not express his feeling of anger over this containment, but kept it within. This information fitted into what the mother later reported.

The remaining parts of this drawing are easier to interpret. The disfigured nose and the elongated neck coincided with the suction tube draining gastric secretions and the tracheotomy. I have already explained other content in the Introduction.

In the case of a forecasting picture, I am frequently asked whether an early diagnosis might have prevented the outcome. This is a Monday-morning quarterback question. After the game, fans can always predict what *should not* have been done and what *should have* been done. I will not be cornered into answering such a question. It could be interesting to explore at some future date, but for now I accept we cannot know the future. Furthermore, I think it would be dangerous to use projective techniques in attempting to predict future events. Yet we can use the picture to forecast, to give an indication to the therapist, to the medical staff and patient as to what areas may need to be explored. If this picture had been given to me at the time it was drawn, I of course would have suggested a physical examination. Had it been determined the child was physically healthy, I would have investigated the psychological implications of containment. I would explore the feelings expressed to see if the energy behind this encapsulation could be reached. Naturally, as a therapist, I would urge expression of this energy. With a five-year-old, we could express this through play, sandplay, theater, or drawings. There are many avenues open to encouraging and aiding this energy to begin flowing. It would not matter which avenue was used—what would matter is that movement was encouraged.

I do not know if an illness can be forestalled by predicting it through pictures. Picture interpretation is an attempt, on my part, to help an individual become more conscious. By becoming conscious, the content within the unconscious may not have to be abused and neglected. It can be respected and integrated into life, and an individual can then live the time he has left as a more whole person, achieving individuality as he sees fit for himself. I can imagine that better health is an outcome of living one's life more completely. Given the interpenetration and connectedness of our psyche and soma, this could well be true. And this is the goal of my writing. Becoming conscious is what this book, and work, is all about. Pictures are tools to help this growth toward consciousness. Perhaps if we each dare to walk one step closer to consciousness, we will live in a more peaceful world, both inwardly and outwardly.

AFTERWORD

have frequently been asked how my interest in drawing interpretation developed. The catalyst was Mr. Heinz, a man I met in Jamaica. He was old, in my eyes, very old. He must have been over eighty-five. At the time I was a Peace Corps volunteer, and I lived and worked in a small village called Wait-A-Bit. My recent graduation from Ohio State University had earned me a degree in education, and I was involved in a teacher training program as a volunteer. We had a few books, and sometimes drawing paper. I believed that drawing provided the manual dexterity, eye-hand coordination, and shape and size differentiation I considered important for these children to learn prior to introducing them to the alphabet.

Mr. Heinz lived just across the road from me. His house was close enough for me to occasionally hear mysterious screams and cries emanating from it. The village had limited electricity, no running water, and our catch-basin was a rain trough with a pipe attached. After many weeks, I met the old gentleman at the "water pipe" and we were able to have a long talk.

I noticed his advanced age and shrunken body. I saw how poor his eyesight was and how shaky and feeble his hands and body movements were.

We initially spoke of my work with the children, my time in Wait-A-Bit, and general small talk. I realized I was going to be late for school,

127

but sensed I was in a more important class with a teacher I could not leave. He asked me to come to his home to meet his wife. I gladly accompanied him to the front of his building, which looked more like a shack than a residence. It was a two-story house, and the lower floor had been a shop in years past. Now it was boarded up and deteriorating. The disintegrating and weather-beaten sides seemed never to have been painted. He asked me to follow him, but we did not enter the house. I noticed a staircase through the doorway. The downstairs did not look livable, and the staircase was useless, with half the steps missing and those that were there shaky in appearance. He couldn't have lived upstairs, so I had to ask myself exactly where he might have lived. We proceeded around to the back, and as we walked I began learning an important lesson.

He told me he was old and was preparing to die. He wanted me to meet his wife, and to see what he still had to do before he died. We dodged some brush, entered a dilapidated mesh wire coop, where a few chickens were kept, and walked to its center. He pointed to the ground and said, "There she is." I looked down and realized we stood upon a cement slab under which was his wife's grave. I wondered to myself if he were a bit "off." He went on to explain to me that he had three wishes before he died, and it was now time to fulfill them. First, he needed to put a proper top on his wife's grave; second, he needed to sell his small plots of land and consolidate his financial resources; and third, he would take the money along with his daughter to the nearby nuns, who would care for her after his death. I was more than a bit jarred. Meeting a grave in a chicken coop, when I thought I had come to meet his wife, having him tell me he was preparing to die, and hearing about a daughter to be given to the nuns, was all a shock. I had not even realized he had a daughter. Neither he nor the community had spoken of her. In my innocence, I thought his preparation for death was not a goal to aim toward but to avoid. But he told me that an old man's needs and views are different from a young man's, and that when I reached his age, I would think differently. I couldn't argue, I was not his age, never had been, and perhaps he was correct.

He took me back to these dilapidated stairs and proceeded to ascend, instructing me to follow carefully. The supporting boards were missing from some steps and I had to walk on the sides and edges, where the beams were, with no guard rail to hold onto. I was twenty-two, he was old and feeble, yet his agility and grace were incredible. I was not at ease, but my curiosity about meeting his daughter kept me going. We walked down a dark narrow hallway to a door. The old man unbolted the door and I stuck my head in, as he told me to do.

The boarded-up windows made it difficult for me to see into the narrow room. There were two chairs, which seemed to have once had round, cane seats. The cane was gone, and there were cans under the chairs. The room had no other furnishings. It reeked, and a woman was crouched in a corner, speaking jibberish, and moaning. I saw that her clothing was soiled and ragged. As I stared into the room I felt a tug on my sleeve and realized it was time to go. The door was rebolted and we climbed down the stairs.

The old man explained that his daughter was in her fifties but had the mind of an infant. He told me she had regressed after a terrible loss of her beloved fiancé. My old friend was planning to give her to the nuns along with his land holdings and money for her "eternal" care. The stone for his wife's grave would be his last purchase.

Like a "good" Peace Corps volunteer, I forged full force ahead in an attempt to rebuild his desire to live. However, as time passed I began to see that for him it was time to move onward. This was difficult to understand from my perspective. This was my initiation to death and dying, and he was my mentor. The impact this experience had on my immature mind was considerable. I decided I wanted to try to understand and assimilate this learning experience. I slowly began to realize that the dying have needs. This man had shared his needs with me. Why had he chosen me? Was there something in me that he sensed? Could I help the dying?

Upon leaving the Peace Corps, I enrolled in graduate school to study counselor education, where I decided to major in work with the terminally ill. I met Dr. Elisabeth Kübler-Ross in 1970 and she encouraged me to look into working with terminally ill children. With my background in education, plus my recent study in thanatology, she suggested that I consider using drawings to work with dying children. She felt this could be a valid means of communication.

Elisabeth encouraged me to read a book written by Susan Bach, which contained two sets of serial drawings from terminally ill children. I read Bach's book and was intrigued. I wrote to Susan Bach in London and made plans to meet her. I began my study by relating with terminally ill adults in an attempt to decipher how these patients could educate the medical staff in ways of better caring for the patient in the dying process. When this study came to an end, I immediately began my thesis study in deciphering the drawings of terminally ill children in an attempt to understand what we can learn from them.

The elements of my experience in the crowded classroom with the drawings from children, plus an old man's perspective and preparation for his death, opened me to Elisabeth's encouragement and guidance to further my quest of learning nonverbal communication.

After receiving my doctorate, I taught at John F. Kennedy University and then decided to return to London to study picture interpretation full-time with Susan Bach. Susan Bach, a Jungian analyst herself, encouraged me to study analytical psychology. She suggested that this would serve to prepare me better to avoid projecting my own psychology (as I had tried to do with Mr. Heinz) into the pictures I was interpreting. For this work I entered the C.G. Jung Institute in Zürich, Switzerland. I selected analytical psychology as developed by Jung rather than other psychologies because Jung taught that a problem is not only a burden to an individual, but it can also be a blessing, and that the blessing may have much to offer in the ongoing life journey. The problems I had faced in my life and in the West Indies became the stepping stones for my ongoing life journey. This school of psychology also recognizes the importance of the symbol to this process, and that the symbol is the healing agent to these burdens and blessings. Today I continue to use drawings with patients at work with their dreams and their illness in connection with a healing process. I also train other therapists in the use of drawings as a healing agent.

Before concluding, I want to add that much of this book is derived from Jung's teachings, from what I have learned in my own analysis, from my teachers Susan Bach and Elisabeth Kübler-Ross, from classes at the C. G. Jung Institute, from myths, fairy tales and legends and from the literature mentioned in the annotated bibliography, as well as from the patients with whom I have worked. I make no claim to own these thoughts or ideas. Much of this work overlaps from one author to another. Yet all of us as therapists must find our own way toward gaining an understanding of picture images. This book is mainly an attempt to organize a systematic approach to communicating with and understanding pictures from the unconscious. To do this I want to remain as close as possible to topics relevant to the interpretation and understanding of pictures from the unconscious.

Frequently in my writing I have been accused of not being assertive enough, of not being certain. For those of you unfamiliar with analytical methodology: when one moves with assertiveness and certainty, little can be known or discovered of the path upon which an individual unconscious travels. I certainly believe our task is to grow toward consciousness. However, growing towards consciousness does not include forcing or directing the unconscious; it includes the task of accompanying the unconscious along its path. "It knows!" With this, I enjoin my colleagues to accompany the unconscious through the use of pictures from the unconscious and learn to become a companion on its very unique way.

A final note on a recent experience—I had the opportunity of returning to Wait-A-Bit. Mr. Heinz had fulfilled his tasks. His wife has a brilliant white tombstone on top of her grave. His daughter died a few months before he did, and their three graves now rest side by side along the ground where the old chicken coop stood. His house is torn down and the vacant lot awaits its new life sometime in the future.

REFERENCE

Bach, Susan. *Acta Psychosomatica: Spontaneous Paintings of Severely Ill Patients*. Geigy S. A., Basel, Switzerland, Printed in Germany, 1969.

Baynes, H.G. & Cary F. *Contributions to Analytical Psychology*. London: Kegan Paul, Trench, Trubner & Co. Ltd., 1928.

Bolander, Karen. *Assessing Personality Through Tree Drawings*. New York: Basic Books, 1977.

Burns & Kaufman. *Kinetic-Family-Drawings* (K-F-D), New York: Brunner/ Mazel, 1970

de Vries, Ad. *Dictionary of Symbols and Imagery*, Amsterdam, Holland: Elsevier Science Publishers, B.V., 1984.

Freud, S. *Totem and Taboo and Other Works*. Collected Works-Volume XIII, London: The Hogarth Press, 1955.

Furth Gregg M. *Impromptu Drawings from Seriously Ill, Hospitalized and Healthy Children: What Can We Learn From Them?* unpublished thesis, Ohio State University, Columbus, Ohio, 1973.

Hammer, Emanuel F. *The Clinical Application of Projective Drawings*. Springfield, Illinois: Charles C. Thomas Publisher, 1980.

Hannah, Barbara, *Encounters With the Soul: Active Imagination*. Boston: Sigo Press, 1981.

Harding, Esther. "What Makes The Symbol Effective As A Healing Agent," *Current Trends in Analytical Psychology*. Gerhard Adler, ed., London, 1961.

Jacks, I. *The clinical application of the H-T-P in criminological settings. In J.N. Buck & E.F. Hammer (Eds.), Advances in the House-Tree-Person technique: Variations & Applications*. Los Angeles: Western Psychological Services, 1969.

Jacobi, Jolande. *Von Bilderreich der Seele. Weg und Umwege zu Sich Selbst.*, Switzerland: Walter-Verlag AG Olten, 1969.

Jacobi, Jolande. *The Psychology of C.G. Jung*. London: Routledge & Kegan Paul, 1980.

Jolles, Isaac. *Catalogue for the Qualitative Interpretation of the House-Tree-Person: HFP* Los Angeles: Western Psychological Services, 1971.

Jung, Carl G. *Collected Works. esp. 4, 5, 6, 7, 8, 13, 16, New York: Pantheon Books Inc., Bollingen Foundation Inc., 1976.*

Jung, Carl G. Man and His Symbols New York: Dell Publishing Company, Inc.,1964.

Jung, Carl G. *Memories, Dreams, Reflections*. recorded and edited by Aniela Jaffe, New York: Pantheon Books, 1963.

Kalff, Dora. *Sandplay*, Boston: Sigo Press, 1980.

Kübler-Ross, Elisabeth, *Living with Death and Dying*, New York: MacMillan, 1981.

Kübler-Ross, Elisabeth, *On Death and Dying*. New York: MacMillan, 1969.

Luscher, Max. *The Luscher Color Test*. New York: Simon & Schuster, 1969.

Shaie, K.W. & Heiss L., *Color and Personality, A Manual for the Color Pyramid Test*, Hans Huber, 1964.

van der Post, Laurens, *The Heart of the Hunter*. London: The Hogarth Press, 1961.

Williams & Furth, 4th Edition, 1985, Privately Published Workshop Manual.

SUGGESTED READINGS
On Drawing Interpretation

Adamson, Edward, *Art as Healing*. London: Coventure Ltd., 1984.
   A series of drawings, paintings, and sculptures collected by a pioneering British art therapist. Although some of the drawings and paintings seem spontaneous or impromptu, most are longer projects, so they cannot technically be looked at in the same way as less structured drawings. Adamson's examples are very well reproduced, and the story of his involvement with art therapy is highly interesting.

Allan, John A.B., "Serial drawing: A Therapeutic Approach With Young Children," (*Canadian Counselor*, 12(4): pg. 223-228, 1978).
   In this excellent paper, the serial drawing technique is described and examples are drawn from two cases. This technique is "generally believed to have stemmed from the C.G. Jung Institute of Los Angeles." Dr. Allen, a Jungian analyst, demonstrates how drawings can "reflect a movement from initial feelings of violence, grief, loss of control, and helplessness to self-disclosure of very painful experiences." The questions: "Why drawing? Why not just talking and listening?" are considered and answered.

Bach, Susan R., *Spontaneous Pictures of Leukemic Children as an Expression of the Total Personality, Mind and Body*, (Schwabe & Co., 1975). (Reprint of an article that appeared in *Acta Paedopsychiatrica*. Vol.41, No.3, 1974/75, Basel, Switzerland, pg. 86-104).
  Three case studies, with accompanying artwork, are presented to illustrate the manner in which such drawings can reveal the patient's "total personality, mind and body, especially at critical moments of life." The quality of the color reproductions of the drawings is quite clear.

Bach, Susan R., *Spontaneous Paintings of Severely Ill Patients*, (Acta Psychosomatica, No.8, Basel, Switzerland: Geigy, 1966).
  Susan Bach has been one of the leaders in the projective use of seriously ill children's drawings as a diagnostic aid. This work, (although out of print, available at most C.G. Jung Institutes), is perhaps the most comprehensive explanation of her work, illustrated by the two cases of Priska and Peter. Extensive chromatic and achromatic drawings accompany each of the two case studies.

Bender, Lauretta, *Childhood Psychiatric Techniques*, (Springfield, IL: Charles C. Thomas Publisher, 1952).
  Bender shows how the drawing of a man by schoolchildren can be used as an indication of possible psychopathology. This work is a fuller presentation of the ideas found in the earlier article, "Art and Therapy in the Mental Disturbances of Children" (Journal of Nervous and Mental Disease, 1937, pg.249-263)

Betensky, Mala, *Self-Discovery Through Self-Expression*, (Springfield, IL: Charles C. Thomas Publisher, 1973).
  Part one of this book consists of ten good case illustrations and studies in art psychotherapy with children and adolescents. Part two is about analytic observations when at work in art psychotherapy. This second part is short and seems incomplete.

Bertoia, Judi and John Allan, "Counseling Seriously Ill Children: Use of Spontaneous Drawings," (*Elementary School Guidance and Counseling*, Feb. 1988, Vol. 22, No. 3, pg. 206-221).
  This article briefly reviews pertinent literature on the child's self-concept and unconscious understanding of the dying process as revealed through art. It provides basic guidelines for eliciting and interpreting children's drawings, giving a theoretical and practical framework. The case study includes ten figures with in-depth interpretation.

Bolander, Karen, *Assessing Personality Through Tree Drawings*, (New York: Basic Books, Inc., 1977).
  Bolander's outstanding work offers a detailed presentation that makes

it perhaps the definitive work on the interpretation of tree drawings. She differs with both Buck (H-T-P) and Koch (the Tree Test)
on some points, and some of her interpretations are regarded as still
speculative, but this work is of tremendous value to clinicians using
drawings with children and adults.

Buck, John N., *The House-Tree-Person Technique (Revised Manual)*, (Los
Angeles: Western Psychological Services,1966).
The validity of the quantitative scoring method used with this projective technique has been questioned by some, but the qualitative section is an excellent description and discusses their possible
interpretations. There are three charts that illustrate many of the
differences seen in drawings. The case studies (with both chromatic
and achromatic drawings) are well presented.

Burns, Robert C. and Kaufman, S. Harvard, *Actions, Styles, and Symbols in Kinetic Family Drawings (K-F-D)*, (New York: Brunner/Mazel,
1972).
A compilation of excellent examples (187) of kinetic family drawings
are provided, with suggestions regarding interpretation and the possible meaning of specific symbols.

Burns, Robert C., *Self-Growth in Families: Kinetic Family Drawings (K-
F-D) Research and Application*, (New York: Brunner/Mazel, 1982).
This book adds new viewpoints to looking at the K-F-D, compares and
contrasts the ways in which the D-A-P, H-T-P, D-A-F and K-F-D portray the self, and shows the results of K-F-D research, including a
computer study of results. Chapters on the depressed and suicidal
child, and on longitudinal studies of self-development, are important additions to the body of work with Kinetic Family Drawings.

Claman, Lawrence, "The Squiggle Drawing Game in Child Psychotherapy,"
(*American Journal of Psychotherapy*, Vol.XXXIV, No. 3, July, 1980).
This eleven-page article is a description of the squiggle-drawing game
as a technique for use with latency-age children. It is an "adapta-
tion of Winnicott's squiggle technique using the story-telling approach of Gardner and Kritzberg."

Dalley, Teresa, ed., *Art As Therapy: An Introduction to the Use of Art
as a Therapeutic Technique*, (London and New York: Tavistock Publications, 1984).
This book aims at introducing the subject of "Art Therapy" to a wide
range of people, including those in the related professions of social
work, psychology, nursing, teaching, and also to those who believe
that "there is more to art than paint on paper."
Some interesting chapters are: Art, psychotherapy and symbol systems;

A Jungian approach to art therapy based in a residential setting;
The use of art therapy in the treatment of anorexia nervosa; Art ther-
apy with the elderly and the terminally ill; Art therapy and prisons;
Art therapy of long-stay psychiatric patients.

Dennis, Wayne, *Group Values Through Children's Drawings*, (New York:
John Wiley and Sons, 1966).
Dennis illustrates the use of drawings as a measure of group social values,
and how content of the drawings is a visual representation of the
values of the group(s) to which the children belong.

Denny, James M., "Techniques for Individual and Group Art Therapy,"
American Journal of Art Therapy, (Spring, 1972).
This seventeen-page article provides a brief overview of many of the tech-
niques in use within the art therapy field. Good resource material.

DiLeo, Joseph H., *Children's Drawings as Diagnostic Aids*, (New York:
Brunner/Mazel, 1983).
Perhaps the most effective presentation to date of technique in interpreting children's drawings. DiLeo illustrates (with over 120 drawings) the many applications of children's drawings and the interpretive
approach used. He also discusses in some detail the errors that are
common among professionals (such as over-interpretation).

DiLeo, Joseph H., *Child Development: Analysis and Synthesis*, (New York:
Brunner/Mazel, 1977).
This work provides an effective overview of theories of child development. DiLeo uses 40 drawings that show how this material can be
used in interpreting children's drawings.

Edwards, Betty, *Drawing on the Right Side of the Brain*, (Los Angeles:
J.P. Tarcher, Inc.,1979).
Aimed at those who are unable to see all that is contained in a drawing, this work (according to Robert Burns and others) goes a long
way toward "overcoming visual illiteracy." The author effectively illustrates the combination of intellectual and emotional components
in drawings.

Freud, Sigmund, "The Moses of Michelangelo," *The Standard Edition*,
(London: The Hogarth Press, Ltd., Collected Works Vol. XIII, 1955,
pg.209-236).
Freud applies a technique that is similar in many ways to the focal points
used in looking at spontaneous or impromptu drawings. Freud believed that by analyzing the emotions aroused in us by viewing a
piece of art, we can gain insight into the emotional attitude in the
artist that impelled him to create that work. The 1914 essay (and 1927

postscript) illustrate an effective way to approach a drawing, and is thus worth consideration by those working in this field.

Furth, Gregg M., "The Use of Drawings Made At Significant Times in One's Life," *Living With Death and Dying* by Elisabeth Kübler-Ross, (New York: MacMillan, 1981).
Five case studies of the use of drawings during "trying times" in one's life. The publisher's quality of the color reproduction in the art work is very poor. For those who are interested in seeing superb color reproductions of this work, see the German edition, *Verstehen was Sterbende sagen wollen*, Kreuzverlag, Stuttgart, Germany, 1982.

Furth, Gregg M., "*Impromptu Drawings from Seriously Ill, Hospitalized and Healthy Children: What Can We Learn From Them*," Unpublished Thesis, Ohio State University, Columbus, Ohio, 1973.
A statistical study comparing the content of pictures between children suffering from leukemia, hospitalized children with non-life threatening illnesses, and healthy children. Case illustrations and pictures (achromatic) are presented. Motif, content shape, size, direction, colors used or not used, suns with a face or not, are some of the variables compared and studied in this research.

Gardner, Howard, *Artful Scribbles*, (New York: Basic Books,Inc., 1980).
The author, a Harvard psychologist, points out the links between a child's drawing and the child's life, from the toddler stage through the adolescent years. The process involved with the work of an adult artist is discussed as well. Gardner acknowledges not only the similarities, but also the important differences in the art produced by different cultures.

Goodenough, Florence, *Measurement of Intelligence by Drawings*, (Chicago: World Book Company, 1926).
This marked the first attempt to measure the intelligence of children according to the number of details the child put into the drawing of a figure of a man. Each drawing is systematically evaluated using a point-scale method.

Hammer, Emanuel F., *The Clinical Application of Projective Drawings*, (Springfield, IL: Charles C. Thomas, 1958).
Hammer's text is now considered a classic and anyone who uses projective tests should be familiar with this work. Buck's House-Tree-Person Technique, Machover's Draw-A-Person Test, and the Draw-A-Person-In-The-Rain Test are a few of the many tests included in this work of 600 pages.

Hulse, Wilfred, C., "Childhood Conflicts Expressed Through Family

Drawings," (*Journal of Projective Techniques*, 16, pg.66-79, 1952).
Hulse states that when attempting to select drawings for this article,
   intrafamilial conflicts varying in form and degree manifested themselves in practically all drawings with so few exceptions that it was
   difficult to select even one which did not have obvious distortions
   and which was relatively free from conflict. He sees drawings as expressing the "language of the dreams" of patients and as significant
   symbolic language in which the unconscious speaks to us. Three cases
   studies are presented.

Hulse, Wilfred C., "The Emotionally Disturbed Child Draws His Family,"
   (*Quarterly Journal of Child Behavior.* Vol. 3, No.2, pg.152-174,1951).
This early paper presents the hypothesis that drawings provide significant clues to intrafamilial conflict. It is the first presentation of
   the technique used by Hulse in which emotionally disturbed children are requested to draw "a family" or to draw "their family." Much
   of this information was later incorporated in the K-F-D of Burns
   and Kaufman.

Kalff, Dora. *Sandplay*, (Boston: Sigo Press, 1980).
This excellent book illustrates "a way of objectifying, in the form of
   symbols, the energy of the unconscious, through the medium of
   sandplay." Mrs. Kalff, a leader in this field and a Jungian analyst,
   presents a creative means of dealing with the issue of personality
   development. Nine interesting case presentations with illustrations
   (achromatic and chromatic) are the thrust of this writing, with an
   opening chapter on "Sandplay: A Pathway to the Psyche."

Kellogg, Rhoda, *Analyzing Children's Art.*, (Palo Alto, CA: Mayfield Publishing Company, 1969).
This work describes the development of art from the two-year old to
   the eight-year old. Although Kellogg focuses primarily upon the
   evolution of the child's art rather than on the child himself and the
   changes he is experiencing which may be symbolically projected into
   his art; she gives generous space to a discussion of Freudian and Jungian theories, as they pertain to art and unconscious functioning.

Kellogg, Rhoda, *Children's Drawings/Children's Minds*, (New York: Avon
   Publishers, 1979).
Rhoda Kellogg, a leader in the field, has examined two million drawings of young children and presents a broad range of them in this
   book. She does so in the attempt to help psychologists become aware
   of the range and scope of children's drawing ability at different age
   levels. "The book is short on words and long on actual child art,"
   so it "can be used as a kind of reference for comparing any given

child's drawings (age 3 to 8) to those of many hundreds of other children; thus we can learn what constitutes 'normal' child art."

Kellogg, Rhoda, *The Psychology of Children's Art*, (CRM, Inc., 1967).
This book, written with Scott O'Dell, looks at the drawings of children ages two to seven from a developmental perspective. Over 250 examples of children's art (most in color) are included.

Klepsch, Marvin and Logie, Laura, *Children Draw and Tell: An Introduction to the Projective Uses of Children's Human Figure Drawings*,(New York: Brunner/Mazel, 1982).
This work offers a brief overview of the theoretical base behind the projective use of art. The four main applications of Human Figure Drawings (H-F-D) are then covered in detail (measure of personality, of the self in relation to others, of group values, and of attitudes). The presentation of the art is most effective, listing the main theme, background data on the child, the overall impression of the drawing, and specific indicators in the drawing that give that impression.

Koch, Karl, *The Tree Test*. (Hans Huber, Verlag, Berne, Switzerland, 1952).
This book provides a detailed account of the development of the test, its standardization, and five case studies. Almost half of the book provides a detailed, clear set of tables illustrating specific interpretations of tree drawings and their components.

Koppitz, E.M., *Psychological Evaluation of Children's Human Figure Drawings*, (Orlando, Fl: Grune and Stratton, Inc., 1968).
Koppitz demonstrates the use of HFDs of children ages five through eleven as a means of measuring intelligence. The system scores the quality of the drawing, unusual items included in the drawing, and the omission of body parts.

Kramer, Edith, *Art as Therapy with Children*., (New York: Schocken Books, Inc., 1977).
An excellent book written by a leader in the field of art therapy. A presentation of a method of working via art with normal, disturbed and handicapped children. It is a " must" for those in the field of art therapy, and is richly documented with case material.

Liebmann, Marian, *Art Therapy for Groups: A Handbook of Themes, Games and Exercises*, (Cambridge, MA: Brooklyn Books, 1986).
This book is for professionals working with groups. It concentrates on how to use art with groups, providing themes for projects, games and exercises. Examples of guided imagery, dreams and meditations are included.

Machover, Karen, "Human Figure drawings of Children," (*Journal of Projective Techniques*, 17, pg. 85-91 1953).
This article builds on Machover's earlier work by studying the drawings (ages five through eleven) of three groups: white, middle-class public school children, black public school children and Jewish private school children. Machover's work, along with that of Buck (H-T-P), forms the basis for most of the work with projective drawings being done today.

Machover, Karen, *Personality Projection In The Drawing of the Human Figure*,(Springfield, IL: Charles C. Thomas, 1949).
Machover showed how drawings could be used as a measure of person ality. They had been used as a measure of development (Good enough) since the 1920's. Machover's theory is that the drawn figure is the subject, and that the paper represents the subject's environment. Of particular interest is the linking of special meaning to specific body parts in the drawings. It is this link that some feel enables these drawings to assist in identifying somatic problems.

Meares, Ainslie, *The Door of Serenity*, (London: Faber and Faber, 1958).
This is "a study in the therapeutic use of symbolic painting." It is a true story with chromatic drawings of two people — the patient and therapist. Drawings are the medium used to bring the patient back to sanity. A very detailed and worthwhile reading.

Milner, Marion, *The Hands of the Living God, An Account of a Psychoanalytic Treatment*, (New York: International Universities Press, Inc., 1969).
This is an account of a schizophrenic woman's twenty-year of analysis with Marion Milner. Dr. Winnicott supervised the lay-analyst author's work, assisted as a consultant and wrote the book's foreword. An interesting book for therapists who are working with schizophrenic patients. One hundred fifty-four black and white drawings with interpretations are included out of over four thousand collected from this one patient. The main theme throughout this writing is the development of a human body-image.

Naumburg, Margaret, *Schizophrenic Art: Its Meaning In Psychotherapy*, (New York: Grune and Stratton, Inc., 1950).
Art productions of two schizophrenic patients are described. It is interesting reading to follow the combined creative and analytic process in these cases, and in one instance the reader can follow a case to the resolution of a serious life problem. A good book to familiarize one with schizophrenic art (achromatic and chromatic).

Reznikoff, Marvin A. and Reznikoff, Helga R., "The Family Drawing Test:

A Comparative Study of Children's Drawings," (*Journal of Clinical Psychology*. No.12, pg.167-169, 1956).

The authors present one of the first studies using Hulse's Family Drawing Technique and present comparative data on boy/girl, black/white, and low/middle income groups concerning their drawings of families.

Rubin, Judith Aron, ed., *Approaches to Art Therapy: Theory and Technique,* (New York: Brunner/Mazel, 1987).

This book is a collection of articles outlining the psychodynamic approaches, humanistic approaches, and behavioral/cognitive/developmental approaches to art therapy. A good reading for art therapists. Its format is divided into three sections: Definition and Orientation to the Particular Theory, The Particular Relevance of the Theory to Art Therapy in General, and finally, Case Examples.

Schildkrout, Molie S., Shenker, I. Ronald, and Sonnenblick, Marsha, *Human Figure Drawings In Adolescence,* (New York: Brunner/Mazel, 1972).

Almost 200 drawings by 12-19 year-olds are included in this work. The authors show how drawings can be an aid in pointing to possible psychopathology. Of special note are the chapters on "Organicity," and "Danger Signals: Acting out, Suicide and Homicide."

Selfa, Lorna, *Nadia : A Case of Extraordinary Drawing Ability in an Autistic Child* (Academic Press, Inc., London, 1977).

A book of interest to those working in the field of mental handicap. A case study of an autistic, six and a half year-old girl with extraordinary drawing ability, showing more that one hundred drawings (achromatic). Gives new insight to reassess our established assumptions about the measurement of intellect, the relationship between perception and learning, and the role of language in formulating concepts.

Shern, Charles R. and Russel, Kenneth R., "Use of the Family Drawing as a Technique for Studying Parent-Child Interaction," (*Journal of Projective Techniques and Personality Assessment*,Vol.33, No.1, pg.35-44, 1969).

The authors report on their use of the Family Drawing technique and note the apparent lack of comment on it in the professional literature (as of 1969). Three case studies are presented with seven drawings reproduced.

Siegel, Bernie, *Love, Medicine and Miracles.*, (New York: Harper & Row, 1986).

Written by a surgeon and professor at the Yale University Medical School, this exceptional book shows how "exceptional patients" survive by, in effect, healing themselves. A handful of drawings is presented, but Siegel's compassion and understanding are a model that should be emulated by anyone involved with ill or dying patients.

Spontaneous Images at Critical Moments of Life: A Contribution to the Relationship Between Psyche and Soma, (in Psychosomatische Medizin, September, 1980).

This is an excellent collection of papers presented in Zurich at a symposium dealing with the diagnostic use of children's art. Included are four presentations by Susan Bach. Some interesting titles by other contributors are: "Spontaneous Process in a Cancer Patient" by Selma Hyman, M.D.; "The First Interview with the Parents of a Fatally Ill Child, and Psychological Follow-up" by W. Hitzig, M.D.; "Personal Experience with a Spontaneous Drawing Reflecting Later Development of An Organic Condition" by H. Desmond, Ph.D. This booklet is available in the United States through Interbook, Inc., New York.

Ulman, Elinor and Dochinger, Penny, *Art Therapy in Theory and Practice*, (New York: Schocken Books, 1975).

This is a collection of readings "whose main emphasis is on diagnosis; studies dealing with the treatment of disturbed children, of the elderly, with schizophrenics, of drug abusers, of the retarded and of troubled families; description of work done in hospitals, community mental health centers, treatment homes, special educational settings and ordinary classrooms."

Virshup, Evelyn, *Right Brain People In A Left Brain World*, (Los Angeles: The Guild of Tutor Press, 1978).

Here we read on how an impromptu abstract design is embellished and eventually "gestalted." It is the integration of mental images which are drawn onto paper along with words. The process is fully described and is made useful for anyone interested in self awareness and for use with patients as well.

Wadeson, Harriet, *Art Psychotherapy*, (New York: John Wiley & Sons, 1980).

An outstanding illustration on how art as a therapeutic tool can be used to treat and gain insight into affective disorders, schizophrenia, neurosis, addiction, and group and family therapy. Opening sections discuss history, philosophy and other fundamentals of art therapy.

Wadeson, Harriet, *The Dynamics of Art Psychotherapy*, (New York: John Wiley & sons, 1987).

This is one in a series of books addressed to behavioral scientists interested in the nature of human personality. It includes chapters on: Encouraging Art Expression; Understanding Art Expression; Relating to Client Around Art Expression, along with Assessment and Beginning Treatment and Mid-Phase and Early Art Therapy Treatment. Several examples are included with over 150 black and white photographs.

Whitmont, Edward C., *The Symbolic Quest*, (Princeton: Princeton University Press, 1969).

Whitmont provides an overall introduction to the basic concepts of analytical psychology, but the material in Chapter One "The Symbolic Approach" will be useful to those who employ projective tests.

Williams, Geraldine H., & Wood, Mary M., *Developmental Art Therapy*, (Baltimore: University Park Press, 1977).

This is an exceptionally valuable resource for those designing a curriculum to promote "sequences of development that foster emotional growth in emotionally disturbed young children. It is based on normal developmental patterns that help children cope effectively with the demands of childhood to develop manipulative, conceptual, social, and communicative skills with children handicapped by emotional or developmental problems."

Williams, Yvonne B., "Reactions to Stress in Cystic Fibrosis Projected in Patients' Drawings; Presented at the Medical/Scientific Conference, Anaheim, California, May 1985, *Caregiver's Paper*, (Rockville, MD: Cystic Fibrosis Foundation Publication, May 1985, pg.31).

An excellent paper explaining and illustrating that cystic fibrosis patients' drawings provide an outlet for expressing grief, anger, frustration, increased tolerance for reality, created by compensatory images; and for integrating experiences and control over anxiety.

Winnicott, D.W., *Therapeutic Consultations in Child Psychiatry*, (New York: Basic Books, Inc., 1971).

Winnicott, the late world-renowned psychoanalyst, describes his use of the squiggle drawing game as a tool in helping children reveal and process conflicts in their lives. He reports on twenty-one case histories—ranging from those with non-psychiatric problems to ones with great psychological complexity and pathology—that demonstrate the value of the squiggle game in promoting communication in children concerning their dreams, phobias, and life experiences. The technique is seen both as a diagnostic and therapeutic aid.

ON AMPLIFICATION OF THEMES

Campbell, Joseph, *The Hero With A Thousand Faces* (Princeton: Princeton University Press, 1972).
This offers a detailed examination of the role of the hero in myth and legend. There is extensive discussion of the three parts of the Quest (separation, initiation, and return). The theme of inactivity before attempting a great task, in preparation for coming trails, is discussed here and had been useful in the analysis of artwork with a client. We are all on a quest, so to speak, and this text is essential for a therapist to understand.

Circlot, J.E., *A Dictionary of Symbols* (London: Routledge & Kegan Paul,1962).
A fifty-five page discussion of symbols, their use and meaning, begins this book. The dictionary section has a limited number of entries, but each of those covered is treated in a comprehensive fashion.

Cooper, J.C., *An Illustrated Encyclopedia of Traditional Symbols* (London: Thames and Hudson, 1980).
This work would be a worthwhile addition to any reference library of symbols and their meanings. The book is excellent and it has the

best cost value when compared with other good symbol books.

de Vries, Ad, *Dictionary of Symbols and Imagery*. (Amsterdam, Holland: Elsevier Science Publishers, B.V., 1984).
This 500 page dictionary is an *excellent* reference for anyone confronted with a search towards better understanding symbols or images. Unfortunately, the cost is outrageous, *the book is superb*.

Grimm's Fairy Tales (New York: Pantheon Books, 1972).
This edition contains the complete Grimm's tales (updated 1942 translation) with an introduction by Padraic Colum, an article by Joseph Campbell and 212 Josef Scharl illustrations.

Heuscher, Julius E., *A Psychiatric Study of Myths and Fairy Tales* (Springfield, IL: Charles C. Thomas, 1974).
Heuscher offers a wide-ranging text that shows where the comparison of dreams, fantasies and hallucinations with folklore can be helpful in recognizing the potential usefulness and meaning of "spontaneous productions of the human psyche." There are numerous parallels between this text and those dealing specifically with spontaneous drawings.

Jacobi, Jolande, *The Psychology of C.G. Jung* (New Haven: Yale University Press, 1973).
Jung himself called this synopsis of his work an insight into his research that "includes all essential points." It has been said by some that the book errs by making Jung too accessible to the lay person and too simple to be true. Nevertheless this is an excellent addition to any reference library.

Jobes, Gertrude, *Dictionary of Mythology, Folklore and Symbols* (New Jersey: Scarecrow Press, 1962).
This work provides the most extensive list of symbolic references available. Originally a three-volume work, it has been pared down to two volumes, but the third volume, a cross-referenced index of symbols, is valuable. Very expensive, though if one works frequently with symbols, it is worth the investment.

Leach, Maria, ed., *Funk and Wagnalls Standard Dictionary of Folklore, Mythology and Legend* (New York: Harper & Row Pub., 1972).
This is an updated one-volume edition of the older slip-cased two volume work. New material has been added and older articles have been trimmed. This work is excellent for professionals, and will be useful to people in many fields.

Nichols, Sallie, *Jung and Tarot: An Archetypal Journey*. (New York: Weiser, Inc., 1980).

This *excellent* work presents a detailed interpretation of the Tarot in terms of analytical psychology. Mrs. Nichols views the "major Arcana as a map outlining the journey toward self-realization." This book is a terrific resource for study and analysis of the drawings of the Major Arcana, and to become familiar with a tremendous volume of symbolism which helps when analyzing and interpreting other drawings.

von Franz, Marie-Louise, *Interpretation of Fairy Tales* (Texas: Spring Publications, 1975).

This text, based on a series of lectures given at the Jung Institute (Zürich) by Dr. von Franz, provides an excellent introduction to work with themes encountered in fairy tales and other unconscious content.

Zimmer, Heinrich, *The King and the Corpse* (2nd edition, Princeton: Princeton University Press, 1956).

Zimmer offers an analysis of some classic motifs that deal with the conflict of good and evil, beginning with a tale from the Arabian Nights. Editor for this book was Joseph Campbell.

The author thanks Bob Stevenson for his help in compiling this annotated bibliography.

Index

abstract, 80, 82-84, 117-118
accident(s), 17-21. *See also* parapraxis
age, trees and, 86-89
analysis/analytical psychology, 9, 15, 88, 108. *See also* Jung
anomalies, 18. *See also* accident(s); odd elements
anger, 95, 109
anxiety, 59-60, 95
Apple Tree Drawing, 86-89. *See also* trees, drawings of
archetypal/archetype(s), 2, 10, 110
art, 12-13, 25, 32
art therapy, 3, 6, 15-26, 56, 101-112, 122. *See also* analysis; therapy
assigned vs. unassigned topics, 24. *See also* impromptu; spontaneous
avoidance, 82

Bach, Susan: *Acta Psychosomatica,* 1, 25, 32, 110
back of drawing, 68-70
barriers, 41-44
Baynes, H.G. & Cary F.:
Contributions to Analytical Psychology, 26
black drawing, 27
Black Sabbath, drawing of, 37-38
boats, drawing of, 57-58
body, in drawings, 1, 51, 54, 60, 121-124
    -mind connection, 23. *See also* psyche and soma
    throat, xv-xvi, xviii
    toe, 53
Bolander, Karen: *Assessing Personality Through Tree Drawings,* 35, 110
breath, xv
burden, 11, 77

carry yourself into the picture, 56-58
cemetery, drawing of, 114-116
central elements, 47-49
Christian(ity), 10
Christmas tree, drawings of, 2-3, 38-39, 64-65. *See also* tree(s)
classifying, 30-31
clouds, in drawing, 95
collective unconscious, 2, 12, 110
color, 95, 97-99, 124
    intensity, 21-22
    out of place, 27, 52, 99-100
commitment, 61
compare to surrounding world, 62-64
compensation/complementary 8-9, 67, 70-71
complex(es), 2-3, 33, 101
conflict, 68, 72-73
conscious(ness), 7-12, 115, 124-125
cultural factors, 62, 97

death revealed in drawing(s), xviii, 55, 60-61, 115, 121
defense mechanisms, 105-106
denial, 79
directions for drawing, 30, 34
Disney character, drawing of, 22-23
distortion, shape, 51-52
dog in drawing, 95
Draw-A-Man, 113
Draw-A-Person, 113
Draw-A-Person-In-The-Rain, 24
drawing(s). *See also* focal points
    assigned vs. unassigned topics, 24.
    See also impromptu; spontaneous
    in black, 27
    of Black Sabbath, 37
    of boats, 57-58
    of body, xv-xvi, xviii, 1, 51, 53-54, 60, 121-124

Studies in Jungian Psychology
by Jungian Analysts

Quality Paperbacks

Prices and payment in $US (except in Canada, $Cdn)

The Secret Raven: Conflict and Transformation
Daryl Sharp (Toronto). ISBN 0-919123-00-7. 128 pp. $16

The Psychological Meaning of Redemption Motifs in Fairy Tales
Marie-Louise von Franz (Zürich). ISBN 0-919123-01-5. 128 pp. $16

Alchemy: An Introduction to the Symbolism and the Psychology
Marie-Louise von Franz (Zürich). ISBN 0-919123-04-X. 288 pp. $20

Descent to the Goddess: A Way of Initiation for Women
Sylvia Brinton Perera (New York). ISBN 0-919123-05-8. 112 pp. $16

Addiction to Perfection: The Still Unravished Bride
Marion Woodman (Toronto). ISBN 0-919123-11-2. 208 pp. $18pb/$25hc

Jungian Dream Interpretation: A Handbook of Theory and Practice
James A. Hall, M.D. (Dallas). ISBN 0-919123-12-0. 128 pp. $16

The Creation of Consciousness: Jung's Myth for Modern Man
Edward F. Edinger (Los Angeles). ISBN 0-919123-13-9. 128 pp. $16

The Analytic Encounter: Transference and Human Relationship
Mario Jacoby (Zürich). ISBN 0-919123-14-7. 128 pp. $16

Change of Life: Dreams and the Menopause
Ann Mankowitz (Ireland). ISBN 0-919123-15-5. 128 pp. $16

The Illness That We Are: A Jungian Critique of Christianity
John P. Dourley (Ottawa). ISBN 0-919123-16-3. 128 pp. $16

Cultural Attitudes in Psychological Perspective
Joseph L. Henderson, M.D. (San Francisco). ISBN 0-919123-18-X. 128 pp. $16

The Vertical Labyrinth: Individuation in Jungian Psychology
Aldo Carotenuto (Rome). ISBN 0-919123-19-8. 144 pp. $16

The Pregnant Virgin: A Process of Psychological Transformation
Marion Woodman (Toronto). ISBN 0-919123-20-1. 208 pp. $18pb/$25hc

Encounter with the Self: William Blake's *Illustrations of the Book of Job*
Edward F. Edinger (Los Angeles). ISBN 0-919123-21-X. 80 pp. $15

The Scapegoat Complex: Toward a Mythology of Shadow and Guilt
Sylvia Brinton Perera (New York). ISBN 0-919123-22-8. 128 pp. $16

The Jungian Experience: Analysis and Individuation
James A. Hall, M.D. (Dallas). ISBN 0-919123-25-2. 176 pp. $18

Phallos: Sacred Image of the Masculine
Eugene Monick (Scranton, PA). ISBN 0-919123-26-0. 144 pp. $16

Touching: Body Therapy and Depth Psychology
Deldon Anne McNeely (Lynchburg, VA). ISBN 0-919123-29-5. 128 pp. $16

Personality Types: Jung's Model of Typology
Daryl Sharp (Toronto). ISBN 0-919123-30-9. 128 pp. $16

The Sacred Prostitute: Eternal Aspect of the Feminine
Nancy Qualls-Corbett (Birmingham). ISBN 0-919123-31-7. 176 pp. $18

When the Spirits Come Back
Janet O. Dallett (Seal Harbor, WA). ISBN 0-919123-32-5. 160 pp. $16

The Mother: Archetypal Image in Fairy Tales
Sibylle Birkhäuser-Oeri (Zürich). ISBN 0-919123-33-3. 176 pp. $18

The Survival Papers: Anatomy of a Midlife Crisis
Daryl Sharp (Toronto). ISBN 0-919123-34-1. 160 pp. $16

The Cassandra Complex: Living with Disbelief
Laurie Layton Schapira (New York). ISBN 0-919123-35-X. 160 pp. $16

Acrobats of the Gods: Dance and Transformation
Joan Dexter Blackmer (Wilmot Flat, NH). ISBN 0-919123-38-4. 128 pp. $16

Eros and Pathos: Shades of Love and Suffering
Aldo Carotenuto (Rome). ISBN 0-919123-39-2. 160 pp. $16

The Ravaged Bridegroom: Masculinity in Women
Marion Woodman (Toronto). ISBN 0-919123-42-2. 224 pp. $20

Liberating the Heart: Spirituality and Jungian Psychology
Lawrence W. Jaffe (Berkeley). ISBN 0-919123-43-0. 176 pp. $18

The Dream Story
Donald Broadribb (Baker's Hill, Australia). ISBN 0-919123-45-7. 256 pp. $20

The Rainbow Serpent: Bridge to Consciousness
Robert L. Gardner (Toronto). ISBN 0-919123-46-5. 128 pp. $16

Circle of Care: Clinical Issues in Jungian Therapy
Warren Steinberg (New York). ISBN 0-919123-47-3. 160 pp. $16

Jung Lexicon: A Primer of Terms & Concepts
Daryl Sharp (Toronto). ISBN 0-919123-48-1. 160 pp. $16

Body and Soul: The Other Side of Illness
Albert Kreinheder (Los Angeles). ISBN 0-919123-49-X. 112 pp. $16

The Secret Lore of Gardening: Patterns of Male Intimacy
Graham Jackson (Toronto). ISBN 0-919123-53-8. 160 pp. $16

Getting To Know You: The Inside Out of Relationship
Daryl Sharp (Toronto). ISBN 0-919123-56-2. 128 pp. $16

Conscious Femininity: Interviews with Marion Woodman
Introduction by Marion Woodman (Toronto). ISBN 0-919123-59-7. 160 pp. $16

The Middle Passage: From Misery to Meaning in Midlife
James Hollis (Houston). ISBN 0-919123-60-0. 128 pp. $16

Chicken Little: The Inside Story *(A Jungian Romance)*
Daryl Sharp (Toronto). ISBN 0-919123-62-7. 128 pp. $16

Coming To Age: The Croning Years and Late-Life Transformation
Jane R. Prétat (Providence, RI). ISBN 0-919123-63-5. 144 pp. $16

Under Saturn's Shadow: The Wounding and Healing of Men
James Hollis (Houston). ISBN 0-919123-64-3. 144 pp. $16

Discounts: any 3-5 books, 10%; 6-9 books, 20%; 10 or more, 25%
Add Postage/Handling: 1-2 books, $3; 3-4 books, $5; 5-9 books, $10; 10 or more, free

Write or phone for free Catalogue of **over 90 titles** and **Jung at Heart** newsletter

INNER CITY BOOKS, Box 1271, Station Q, Toronto, ON M4T 2P4, Canada
Tel. 416- 927-0355 / Fax 416-924-1814 / E-mail info@innercitybooks.net